STORIES Y MISFIT

STORIES of an ORDINARY Misfit

by Tim Haynes

Published by:
MISFIT Publications.

First published in:
South Africa in 2015.

Second Edition in:
Malaysia in 2015

ISBN 9780620655484
9 780620 655484

ISBN: 978-0-620-65548-4

Edited:
Jane Fox.

Design, typography & some photographs:
© Brian Whitehead in London.

Printed and produced by:
Subuhani Hamzah in Malaysia.

Some names in this book are the real names of people some of whom are still kicking. Some names are pseudonyms assumed by, or given to people. Their real names were never known to me. I myself had two names. People know one or another version of me. Kurtz, Conrad's protagonist in 'Heart of darkness' was known to have been a few real people combined into one. In this book all the people are versions or combinations of people. Therefore any similarity to any person living or dead, is purely in the mind of the reader.

There is also a digital edition available on demand from the email address below:

tim@geza.co.za

STORIES of an ORDINARY Misfit

Tim Haynes:

Was born in Johannesburg South Africa and received some education at King Edward VII School and Witwatersrand University.

He moved to Cape Town for a short while, before emigrating to London, England.

After fourteen years he moved to County Kerry in Eire with partner Clare and their son Ciaran.

They lived in the remote countryside for four years where daughter Gina was born.

In 1994 the family returned to Johannesburg South Africa where they still live today.

Tim Haynes wrote a first book entitled ***'The House at the Edge of the World'****, a story of the four years spent in the Irish backwoods.*

He is contactable through email at:
tim@geza.co.za
or on Facebook.

Acknowledgements:

Without the badgering of Piers Cross, I would not have joined Jane Fox's writing group. To do so was a seminal moment in my writing life.

Not only has Jane and her group changed my writing in the subtlest of ways. They have pointed out my weaknesses and excesses, and at the same time encouraged my story telling strengths. Jane Fox also edited this book. It wasn't easy.

I met Dawn Garisch, a writer and memoir teacher in Cape Town, who kindly read some of this work and convinced me that it was a project worth seeing through. She described it as LOL stuff, which is what it is meant to be, so I knew I was on the right track.

If Brian Whitehead, an old friend residing in London, hadn't been so supportive of the telling of these stories, it wouldn't have happened. He followed this up by using his talent as a graphic designer and typepographer to lay out the book and provided many of his own pictures from those taken at the time. Thank you seems totally inadequate.

Many others were readers and critics along the way, vital contributors to a writer's need to keep plugging away. Thanks to Gil Brokensha, Deborah Choate, Piers Cross, Merlynn Edelstein, Cuz Jeppe, Melody Emmett, Kay Brown, Lisa Swart, Douglas MacCutcheon and all others at the writing group as well as Geoff Foote and Philippa Kennedy in England.

And of course, Clare, my partner, who has heard these stories a million times and was still able to stay enthusiastic, and Ciaran and Gina, who also had to go through the hard times with me.

INDEX.

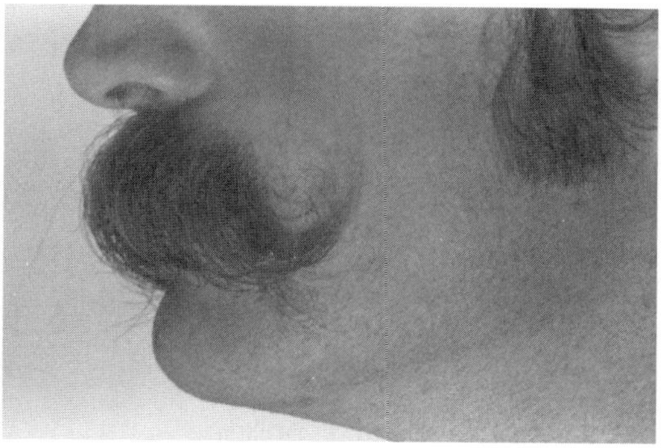

STORY 1

OTHERWISE JUVENILE.

When I was twelve years old and in my final year at preparatory school, I was a big shot. I was vice-head prefect, I was captain of the cricket team and the first soccer team. But then my parents went on an extended overseas trip and shipped in Uncle Abe and Aunty Joyce to look after us four kids. They were childless and out of their depth. Uncle Abe polished his Mercedes in the yard and Aunty Joyce did her immaculate hair and nails. The wheels came off. From then on, I was a naughty boy.

Towards the end of that year, after a succession of misdemeanours at school, I was sent off to the headmaster's office. He told me I had been the biggest disappointment to him in his long and illustrious career in the education profession. Three days later he died. The story was that he had slipped in the bath, hit his head, had a stroke and perished.

Of course the whole incident shook me up a bit at the time, even though at twelve I had no real life experience. The comprehension of death was beyond me. I remember my overwhelming reaction to this tragic event was: 'well I'm never going to change his mind now'.

I made my way through the high school years with one infraction after another under my belt. In my final year I should have been one of the leading lights, as I seemed to have all the potential in the world, but again, I fell short. Not as a result of lack of talent, rather from an intuitive awareness of the fallibility of others, in this case the teachers and the headmaster. I also had an aversion to the school traditions. These all made me a premature sceptic. At best, I then deliberately pushed the boundaries. At worst, naughtiness morphed into rebellion.

In those days the school had a large percentage of Jo'burg Jewish kids as pupils who were definitely not the rugger buggers. And because I lived in Observatory, my mates were Jews from Yeoville, Berea and Hillbrow, whose fathers owned small businesses such as car repair garages. My social milieu already consisted of a bunch of sceptics, due to them being too close to the wrong side of the wealth tracks.

In my final years of high school the headmaster lived in a cut sandstone school house in the old English style, appropriate to his position. He was having an affair with a pupil's mother. She lived in a small flat only a block away from our family house. I knew her well because I fooled around in the road with her son. Her husband had died some years before, so for her the affair was all kosher. Not so for him, with his family back home. We are talking 1969 here, when these things were more under wraps than they are now. Every morning on my way to school, I walked past his grey Ford Zephyr parked outside the flat, and my schoolboy mind would run wild. Our headmaster humping away? Nah, couldn't picture it. I would report to my tjommies the latest developments which elicited much mirth as their juvenile minds ran as rampant as mine. The moral messages inherent in the headmaster's assembly sermons were somewhat negated by the glances and smirks shared between us learners, gathered like sheep down on the floor before him.

I was enough one of the star pupils to be included in a silly stunt dreamed up by the rugger buggers to punish our hated science teacher.

For what? Well, in defence of the indefensible, he was an unpleasant man. His modes of discipline were laughable, his breath was foul, he spoke funny, he had large protruding ears and walked in a peculiar way. All grist to the mill of a spiteful bunch of unruly boys. We went to his house in the middle of the night, pulled down his rickety front fence and dug up his roses. In time we were bust by a boy who thought his reward might be ascension to the head prefect role. It wasn't. The story even made the newspapers. One by one the headmaster interrogated the perpetrators. The head prefect got the chop, he demoted the other prefects (I was one), and two others got six of the best. One claimed that he got seven. During my interrogation I told him that I agreed it was an abominable incident, that it was dreamed up by the rugger buggers and that I only went along because of peer pressure. I added that being a prefect was galling to me, because I was forced to be part of the rugger buggers' system of dominance and that I was pleased to be shot of it now. The headmaster was impressed by my speech. He told me I'd obviously read Dale Carnegie's How to win friends and influence people and that he would explain to my father how it was that I was unfortunately involved. I thanked him. I hadn't read Mr Carnegie, in fact I'd never heard of him. But I had been strategising with my Jewish mates.

A mere two weeks later I was at it again. My gang of four decided to go to the Jo'burg drive-in next to Alexandra Township. A car was a pre-requisite for a visit to a drive-in, and we were sixteen-year-old school boys. Charles Hoddes lived in Highlands North; his father's car was housed in a garage that opened onto the street. His father was a short, bald, thickset man named Sonny. I never heard Sonny speak one word. He disappeared into his bedroom at 8:00 pm like clockwork every night, not to re-emerge until the next day's morning departure for work.

The four of us relieved the kitchen keyboard of the car keys, and silently freed Sonny's Fiat Lada from the confines of the garage. We pushed the vehicle out of earshot of the house before we had it roaring to life. I was at the wheel, being the only competent driver. We headed off. Barry Levy insisted that he have a go at the wheel, promising the rest of us that he too could drive. He took off down the slope of Johannesburg Road at a fair lick, unaware of the S-bend rapidly approaching. He shouted excitedly, 'I'm in fourth,' as we hit the S-bend. Out of control the car rolled over and over onto a vacant lot, mercifully a flat piece of veld. It came to a halt - on its side. There was silence. Dust rose eerily, engulfing the car. A collective stillness of the jumbled bodies inside the vehicle spoke of wonderment at whether we'd died and arrived in heaven, or were about to experience some hell on earth. We scrambled through the smashed windows at the top of the car. Miraculously there were no injuries. When the dust had settled, we pushed the car over onto its wheels. The roof and doors were stoved in, the straw of the veld was sticking to the tyres. We got back in the car, put the key in the ignition and it started. We put it in gear and it moved. Gingerly we drove it back to its home, and pushed it silently into the garage.

I pleaded with the boys: I wasn't the driver, it wasn't 'my' car, I had just been in deep kak of my own at school, so leave me out. Ian Berman similarly took the coward's route and slunk home quietly leaving Barry and Charles to face the music. They decided not to wake Sonny from his slumber that evening. He would need all his energy to cope with this unpleasant surprise the following morning. Sonny awoke, went through his early morning routine, the one he'd been following for thirty years with still fifteen to go before retirement. He plucked the car-keys from the board and went through to the garage. A silence of disbelief, of non-comprehension followed. The boys, lying silently in bed unable to sleep, had spent the night contemplating this moment. Then a noise came out of Sonny which was not human. It swept down the passage like a twister, found the cowering boys and visited upon them a horror both physical and vocal. Even today, forty years on, they are unable to laugh about it.

Life in Jo'burg for adolescent kids in those days was a constant search for some form of entertainment, and the pursuit became especially manic on a Saturday night. Private parties were a problem because of fighting usually between rival gangs. The synagogues had socials, but even they were few and far between. We had to make up our own entertainment. Our particular stomping ground was Hillbrow. Although the clubs were still beyond our age reach, we would choose a large block of flats and walk the passages until we came across a party - or something. It was completely unpredictable, it was often out of our league. And once you were in sometimes it was hard to get out. But it was entertainment.

This diet of fun was occasionally broken. The newspaper reported on the upcoming World Title fight between World Champion wrestler, Hungarian Josci Molnar and the legendary Jan Wilkens in the Jo'burg City Hall. We had been informed that spectators at this sport had to arm themselves with eggs and tomatoes, in case the battle should disappoint. We purchased 4 cheap seats in the gallery where we joined a couple of hundred bus conductors who were coming off shift right there at the bus terminus in the middle of town. Josci and Jan paraded the world champion's belt up for grabs that night, and did battle, a closely fought contest which Josci narrowly won. The bus conductors in the gallery were incensed, Jan Wilkens was their man and he was robbed. Josci was provocatively parading the belt. We opened up the plastic hold-alls and let fly the eggs and tomatoes. We were surprised that we were the only ones. They spattered on the corner of the ring and over Josci in his white silk gown and his shining gold belt. He looked up, saw from whence the stuff was coming, the aperture in his bald head stretched open, gold teeth framed a blue tongue and the froth of flying spittle as he began wading through the crowd in an effort to get to us. The bus connies were delirious with excitement, howling with laughter and clapping us on the back. We decided it would be prudent to hot foot it out of there before Josci could get anywhere near us.

†††

I was an officer in the school cadet corps. My second in command was Mark Stein, my good friend and neighbour in Observatory and the naughtiest boy in the school. We commanded fifty junior boys in the platoon. It was usual for officers to take responsibility for discipline in the ranks. In this case the officers, Mark and I, took it upon ourselves to amuse the troops. On the big day of the year, the South African Defence Force bigwigs came out to judge the performance of the cadets - our performance. On the school rugby field, the march past the makeshift podium began. The top brass, with uniforms ironed to perfection and badges of decoration glinting in the bright sun, were taking the salute. Our platoon was in the forefront with many others following in our footsteps behind. I gave the command Left Turn. It should have been Right. Our platoon went marching into the rugby stands in disarray, followed by 700 others. It was a disaster, I was the disaster.

†††

I was bunking with regularity. Once I nipped around the corner to Mark Stein's house for a quiet day at home. It was safe there, both his parents worked. An hour later a knock on the door signalled a visit by the vice-headmaster of the school paying home visits to all those matriculants who were playing truant. I hid away while Mark played the home alone sick child. I knew that the vice head would be visiting my house soon if he hadn't already done so. When the coast was clear, I nipped home, making sure that nobody saw me. We lived in a double story residence, my bedroom was the only one on the ground floor. I sneaked into the house undetected by my mother or 'the help', and dived under the bed-covers. Not five minutes later there was a knock at the door and my mother opened it to the same vice head who asked my whereabouts. My mother told him I'd gone to school as usual. Bingo. The vice head was proud to announce that I wasn't at school and that the matter would be taken up accordingly. He was so chuffed with himself that he used some loose words like 'dishonesty', 'irresponsibility', 'lack of integrity'.

Later in the day when my mother was passing my room, I groaned loudly. She came to investigate. I told her I tried to go to school, but was struck down by a disintegrating stomach which I'd been painfully emptying the entire morning. My mother went straight to the phone and laid into the vice head for his opinion of me when I was suffering sick as a dog at home in bed. 'No integrity? Dishonest? My son? It's an outrage, Mr Armstrong.' I heard her putting down the phone. At her eightieth birthday in my speech I recounted the story, the truth had never been divulged before. She didn't smile, just made a tisk noise with her tongue.

On another occasion I spent the day at one of the gang of four Ian Berman's place of abode in Hillbrow. He resided at the Lloyd residential hotel. My girlfriend at the time bunked in solidarity. She and I spent most of the day alone in the bedroom (with not much progress made), except that we did have our kit off with the other lads outside trying to catch a glimpse through the keyhole. It came time to leave and we thought it quite fun if I wore her clothes and she wore mine, both denims and t-shirts. We walked down to Louis Botha Avenue, Clarendon Circle to hitch a ride home, quite easy and common in those days. The first person to stop was my father. He lifted Clare Bowers (whose father was a gynaecologist colleague of his) all the way home to Waverley before returning back to Observatory. Nothing was said on that trip by anybody. It was an uncomfortable hour.

After our final matriculation exam, it was Ian Berman* who announced... 'right boys, it's party time.' We made our way down to the 'sewerage farm' - the woods near Birnam. He had already prepared some dagga joints. I thought 'well this is it, I'm no longer a school kid, this is what having a good time is going to be all about'. I was up for it and inhaled on those joints with carefree abandon. We walked on to a burger bar in Corlett Drive. I felt no different, and disappointment was just setting in when I noticed, with my own eyes, the tomato sauce bottle (or was it the mustard?) levitating above the table. I never saw the world in quite the same way again.

My misbehaviour in that final school year had no limits. The end result was very poor matriculation grades. My father, by now a professor of surgery at the university, had his work cut out swinging a place for me in the Faculty of Building Science. This faculty was new, trying to get students in. None of the others would have me. There was no say in the matter, nor honestly, did I have much interest. My father had escaped the poverty of his childhood, caused by his father's radical politics and rebellion, by a will and effort that was truly admirable and momentous. He had taken himself with his family decisively into the heart of the professional classes. He was an ear, nose and throat surgeon before retiring to academia and the first chair for this subject at the University of the Witwatersrand. He had escaped the poverty trap through blood sweat and tears, and here was I his son, born into comfort and well-being with no understanding or appreciation of what it had taken for me to be there.

University was the road that my father knew to take to get out of the ghetto, it was the road he wanted me to take to stay out of the ghetto. So of course I had to go to university.

†††

A huge influence was my older brother Terence. He was nineteen in 1967 and had just completed one year of army service in Pretoria. As a kick-off to his further middle class education, my father kindly sent him on a European tour. One stop-over location was definitive in his life: London. London in 1967 was Carnaby Street, psychedelic fashion, drugs, music, free love, make peace not war, we'll make a revolution, hippie-dom gone berserk. My brother was more than touched by the whole experience.

He returned from London with several interesting things in his kit. One item was life changing. It was a large picture poster. My father, a pillar of society, returned from work and was informed of a new objet d'art on Terence's bedroom wall. He paid the room a visit and was confronted by a black and white poster - not of pop-art, all the rage just then - but of Jimi Hendrix, in full hippie regalia, naked from the waist up. Afro, animal tooth necklace, bandana AND smoking a spliff, the smoke curling lazily up from the corner of his mouth.

My father went ballistic. We are talking Johannesburg, South Africa, in Johannes Balthazar Vorster's time. A half-naked black man smoking ganga on the wall. My brother stood firm. My father stood firm. My father and brother never again communicated in any way other than with acrimony, until Terence had finished his degree (in accountancy) and left to live in London.

Terence taught himself to play the guitar, as did many kids in imitation of Joan Baez, Bob Dylan and others. In his student days Terence became a minor pop star around Jo'burg, playing the clubs and bars. Bob Dylan was the spokesman for this generation, and Terence regularly covered this track…

†††

Come mothers and fathers throughout the land
And don't criticize what you can't understand
Your sons and your daughters are beyond your command
Your road is rapidly aging
Please get out the new one if you can't lend a hand
For the times they are a-changing.

On the sidelines I, the younger brother, was standing by watching it all play out around me.

†††

My first year of university was spent in a state of puzzlement. Of trying to find out how things worked, what was going on in the world, in life and in my head. My real education had to start somewhere. The music, style and consciousness created principally by the new pop culture of that time had given young people of my ilk something far from the stifling values and lifestyle of our parental generation. It was something exciting that belonged to the youth, so much ours that our parents were opposed on that count alone, and that contributed to the appeal. And especially in South Africa, where repression was prescribed by law.

The sum total of my formal learning thus far was that I could read, write and was numerate, with a bit of sport and delinquency thrown in. The rest was rubbish. History as put out by the Nationalist Government education system? ...Nah! Afrikaans – given what it represented... definitely not! Was the rest of the world an enemy who wanted our destruction? I didn't think so. Were black people an underclass, sub-human, to be kept in pens without identity? No. There was something wrong with this version of the world and maybe even there was something wrong with the world as it really was. I decided to experience whatever alternative I could lay my hands on. And if the powers that be - my parents, the government- banned it, so much more important that it should be investigated. That was my first year at university. It wasn't so much Witwatersrand University, it was life.

So what was on offer for those with receptive minds? In hindsight, I sat down to research some life experiences and influences from the late 60s and 70s. The choice for a generation of uncertain young people at that time was stupefying. To satisfy the new demand, religions were hastily

Mark Gevisser makes a most interesting and important point, in his description of the white Jo'burg experience in his book 'Lost and Found in Johannesburg', that whites who opposed Apartheid had to quantify what they would forfeit, 'alongside the gains of moral purpose,' unlike the black populace who had nothing to lose.

Four years later, under the influence of serious drugs, Ian Berman jumped out of the window of a high-rise block of flats in Hillbrow to his death.*

being concocted, or rehashed versions of the old were being taken out of the cupboard and given a dusting. With slogans abounding like 'The personal is the political', it was show-time for any charlatan.

When the Beatles went off barefoot to meet the Maharishi Yogi, it represented a massive leap into mind expansion and the extension of freedom. It was a statement of intention to investigate foreign things, spiritual things, and things from outside the western white diaspora. Maharishi Yogi, the man credited with the popularization of the Transcendental Meditation technique, prided himself in not having the same obsession with Rolls-Royces as some of his contemporaries, such as Bhagwan Shree Rajneesh of the 'orange people'. He was happy with a much smaller fleet and a single helicopter. Strange for a man who put 'yogic flying' on the menu of necessities for the world populace to learn, before world peace was possible. Practitioners of yogic flying have described three stages to the art. Hopping, floating and flying. The hopping stage has been described as the body moving forward, with crossed legs in small jumps. Floating and flying come with the perfection of hopping. It is not possible to attain a flying consciousness sitting cross legged on the floor. I've tried it. It would have made more sense to advise jumping off a cliff or high rise building, but even that is difficult starting in the lotus position. It is not surprising that floating and flying have never been witnessed, and the Maharishi himself once told Paul McCartney that he had never levitated, or witnessed anyone else levitating, let alone flying or floating.

The Maharishi died in 2008 having inspired the anti-materialism of the 1960's. He amassed a fortune estimated to be as much as 5 billion dollars.

†††

There was the Guru Mahara Ji. I went to a weekend camp in a beautiful fruit growing area called Elgin in the Cape Province of South Africa. The camp was a numbers building and mind expanding exercise put on by the then dynamic and growing Guru Mahara Ji's movement (South

African chapter). Ji himself was also growing, he was only fourteen at the time, having assumed leadership of the movement at six years old, imparting wisdom as only a six-year-old can. He was physically growing too, his fat little body unable to resist all those burgers and cream buns which he religiously ordered, and who would dare to question his dietetic habits when he was instructing people on world peace. All the camp 'supervisors' had beautifully exotic names of Indian origin, but their hues and accents were unashamedly white middle class South African. We played many games aimed, I think, at mind expansion, certainly stuff I'd never experienced before. One memorable exercise was when we were blindfolded, then paired off with a member of the opposite sex. We had to then think up a name for ourselves that we would have liked to have had as our own, and then confess it to our 'partner'. I desperately wanted to participate without cynicism, to do things right just for once without taking the piss. But I could genuinely not think of a name for myself. And then in my mental frenzy, the name 'Errol Flynn' came up and wouldn't be dislodged. He was a popular film star of the 40s, who had a reputation as a womaniser and from whom the expression 'in like Flynn' was coined. All way before my time.

I remembered my seven-year-old school friends and I discussing sex. We were adamant that the penis should be inserted straight into the belly button, after all there was no other hole in sight. The conversation moved on to talking about Errol Flynn who must have been in the news at that time. Somehow Errol was famous not as a film star, but as a man who'd killed several woman with his huge dick, so the kids said. I realized then that I'd never checked the story, either about the size or the killing, and time was running out. Without alternative I blurted out 'Errol Flynn' to my silent blindfolded partner. She told me her name was Ursula Andress, just recently dressed only in a towel over the shoulders in the film 'The Blue Max'. When Errol Flynn heard that he rose, as if from the grave, for one last hurrah. The masks came off, Errol Flynn bearded with long blonde flowing locks and hard on and Ursula Andress short fat dumpy kugel with freckles and big thick tortoise shell glasses over a huge nose. That was my first real (unsuccessful) name changing experience, and for me the most memorable part of the Guru Mahara Ji enlightenment.

The Guru Mahara Ji gave up the whole thing in his early twenties when his mother said he could not marry an American woman and move to the States. He defied his old mum, married the American woman, moved to the United States and got a job in insurance.

†††

Chandra Mohan Jain, another Indian, became Bhagwan Shree Rajneesh and eventually ran an ashram of 10,000 devotees in Oregon, USA known as the 'orange people'. He amassed more than $100 million and a fleet of Rolls Royces while preaching a doctrine of sexual freedom and mysticism. With 10,000 voters in one small locale, he could dominate local political power. The cultists hatched a poisoning plot, intending to incapacitate non-sect voters. 750 people were poisoned in Oregon in 1984 by infecting a series of salad bars with salmonella. In 1986 two top cultists pleaded no contest to the poisonings and other charges, and were sentenced to twenty years in prison. The attack was the worst bio-terrorism assault on US soil. Of course old Chandra was nowhere to be found. He had secretly fled back to India, where he died in 1990.

†††

Years later, Salman Rushdie (in Joseph Anton) told Meg Ryan of his scepticism regarding the guru industry… 'Why are you so cynical?' she asked him. He said that if you grew up in India it was easy to conclude that these people were fakes. 'Yes of course there are lots of charlatans,' she said reasonably, 'but can't you discriminate?' He shook his head sadly. 'No,' he said. 'No I can't.' And that was the end of their chat.

These movements, and many others which were less successful, had one thing in common. They were led by power hungry charismatic dictators, those that formed and controlled them. They were skilled in understanding how to appeal to the dissatisfied youth. But they were essentially not different from Charles Manson or Jim Jones. The difference was in the degree of megalomania.

Charles Manson encouraged his (mainly female) followers to hack into little pieces the beautiful people, the then Hollywood celebs, Sharon Tate (Roman Polanski's wife) being the most famous. Such was his power over the psyche of his followers, assisted by drugs and alcohol, that when their appalling murders were executed Manson himself was not even there.

Manson himself ascribed the real driving force of his deeds as coming from the Beatles. It was the White Album, and in particular the track Helter Skelter, together with copious amounts of drugs and alcohol that got the psychopath in him going. The girls didn't like how they had been brought up, didn't like the world they had been brought into, were not going to succumb to it, believed that Manson offered a more attractive option, and were going to make a new world in his image. Just a small-time, home-brew guru.

The most tragic of those that combined religion and politics was Jim Jones. Unlike almost all the other charlatans, he didn't even change his name.

Jones started out deeply religious before his membership of the Communist Party in America, reading the writings of Stalin, Marx, Gandhi and Hitler. Up to the sixties Jones always emphasized the social values of religion, but through the sixties he was open in his 'apostolic socialism' teachings. He had long since come to realize that the way to achieve social change through Marxism in the United States was via religion. After all wasn't religion 'the opium of the people'? Even so, his considerable following by 1976 created the confidence in him to throw off his religious shackles and call himself an atheist. Jones built Jonestown in Guyana to be a benevolent communist community stating ...'I believe we're the purest communists there are.'

He was arrested in 1973 for soliciting a man (who happened to be a cop) for sex in a movie theatre near Macarthur Park in Los Angeles. Jones banned sexual activity amongst his Temple members outside of marriage, while he voraciously engaged in sex with both male and female members of his Temple. He claimed that he only engaged in homosexual activity with male Temple adherents for their own good and to connect them symbolically to him. He fathered more than one child with temple disciples.

Many family members of the disciples back in the USA became concerned about the turn of circumstance at the ranch in Guyana. Their complaints of human rights abuses to the US government resulted in a fact finding mission by American congressman Leo Ryan to the Jonestown ranch in Guyana in 1978. Jones' paranoia went into overdrive, resulting firstly in the shooting dead of Ryan and then the massacre of 909 men, women and children by cyanide poisoning which was the largest mass suicide/ killing of people in history, and the greatest loss of life in an unnatural disaster in American history up to that point in time. Leo Ryan, the American congressman, has gone down in history as the only American congressman assassinated in the line of duty.

†††

Philip Roth in The Dying Animal writes '...This was not a pretty revolution taking place on a dignified theoretical plane. This was a puerile, preposterous, uncontrolled, drastic mess, the whole society in a huge brawl... People took off their underwear and walked around laughing. Often it was no more than farce, childish farce, but astonishingly far reaching childish farce... Yet the impact was revolutionary. Things changed forever.'

†††

Meanwhile, on a macro scale, resistance to America's war in Vietnam was growing. There were student riots and anti-war protests in the USA (students in Europe too were in a state of discontent.) In the face of this discontent, the Yanks then created the biggest monster of them all. Not back in the USA mind you, not even in Vietnam, but in Cambodia.

In 1973, as fast as the US was dropping half a million tons of bombs on Cambodia, a country they were not even at war with, the Khmer Rouge was recruiting peasants in the countryside who were understandably upset by the Yankee onslaught. One day they were quietly going about tending their rice paddies in order that they could eat, and the next, bombs instead of raindrops were falling from the sky. Khmer Rouge recruited on a ticket of anti-production/consumer society, anti-people who use their wealth, their resources, their brainpower to obliterate harmless defenceless peasants growing their vegetables in their own backyard. In 1975 the peasant army of Pol Pot captured the capital Phnom Penh. The Khmer Rouge subjected Cambodia to a radical social reform process that was aimed at creating a purely agrarian-based communist society, the opposite of America's. The city dwellers were educated civilians from urban areas, and therefore no good at working in fields, to which the Khmer rouge applied the motto 'To keep you is no benefit. To destroy you is no loss.' They were deported to the countryside where they were subjected to forced labour. Up to three million Cambodians (out of 7.5 million) are estimated to have died or been killed in waves of murder, torture, starvation, aimed particularly at these educated and intellectual elites from the towns. Their crime – they resembled Americans.

And for the young, for people like me, getting angry, once again it was Bob Dylan addressing these Masters of War:

Come you masters of war...
...I hope that you die, and your death will come soon
I'll follow your casket on a pale afternoon,

I'll watch while you're lowered, down to your deathbed
And I'll stand by your grave to make sure that you're dead.*

I had learnt much in my first year of university. And unbelievably, miraculously, I passed my exams. Building Construction 1, Theory of Structures 1, Mathematics 1, Quantity Surveying 1, Building Science 1 were my credits.

†††

There were very few left field thinkers doing Building Science. Then someone's older brother invited me and a group of mates on a SAVS camp. SAVS, the South African Voluntary Service, was an organization that built useful structures like class rooms or clinics in the homelands, in the townships of South Africa, on weekends and uni vacs. And we were looking for an escape from that desperately boring safari suit existence that was the politics and life of Johannesburg. We still lived at home. Not yet had we escaped to our first commune, or as my mother called them …'combine'. So SAVS it was that gave us the first 'out'. It was an organisation on campus that suited our budding building talents and that persuaded us that maybe learning about building did have a useful function.

SAVS was happy to have us, precisely because of our growing expertise in building. They had an oversupply of philosophy and politics students. So we started on the SAVS camp, and within a short space of time we were SAVS, and we were the SAVS camp. I went on camps in Fascadale, St Faiths and Dundee in Kwazulu Natal, I went all over Lesotho and Magaliesburg and Bronkhorstspruit. For me the lecture theatres of the building science department at university had receded into irrelevance.

I led a camp to Thaba Bosiu in Lesotho in the winter of 1973. We were to build three classrooms and four teachers' accommodation rooms in the shadow of King Moshoeshoe's famous flat top mountain fortress. Twenty students (half male, half female) from the northern suburbs of Jo'burg, used to all the mental and material comforts that apartheid living could dish up, were now sleeping on a concrete floor in the icy Lesotho mid-winter. There was no running water except in the river, a mile away, and even colder than chilly. Those that chose to mix concrete, erect makeshift scaffolding, lift and lay concrete bricks did so. Those that chose to cook, clean and do chores of assistance did so.

The nights were a party as only students can party. People brought guitars, made drums, the locals came down from the village and it was raucous revelling. For everyone it was a journey of discovery about a different life from that which they knew. And it was confirmation that what we were thinking about the world and about South Africa was not wrong, was not some misguided mumbo jumbo, was not unrealistic. We were not alone. We were at one with the most important constituency of all – our peers. The education wasn't academic, it was real. And it laid down markers about all facets of our lives. At first it was just a different thing to do in the vacation. But it was seminal. Everybody returned with a modified attitude to life from the one they'd arrived with. I have met people forty years after being on one of those camps, and they still talk of the life-changing nature of that experience.

For me it was pivotal. It was like all those years of not knowing what was the cause of my frustration and rebellion, I had started to find a reason. It wasn't only me. The world was a mess, especially South Africa. I had started to find an outlet.

An ideological battle then took place between us all in SAVS. It was about building structures, even useful structures, in the homelands. The people didn't want to be in a homeland, the people didn't want to learn what the Nationalist government wanted to teach them. The debate split the organisation. Some of the students went overseas, some others joined more radical organisations. The next intake assumed control of SAVS. It was probably what had happened several times before - the passing of the baton. But the term 'working class' had entered the fray. I could strum a tune on the guitar. At those SAVS camps it was mandatory for even the guitar to be passed around communally. I played my anthem, night in night out. The tune that was played on that guitar every evening was John Lennon's Working Class Hero:

> ***...There's room at the top they're telling you still***
> ***But first you must learn how to smile as you kill***
> ***If you want to be like the folks on the hill***
> ***A working class hero is something to be***
> ***If you want to be hero well just follow me***

†††

Protest was spreading to every facet of life. One didn't have to be 'into politics' to be touched by it. Even in sport one could not help but be touched by protest never heard of before. Cassius Clay became Muhammed Ali and went to jail instead of Vietnam when he was World Heavyweight Champion. He was followed by the black American sprinters who shocked the world with their fisted salute of protest against racism on the podium of the Olympic games. Terrorists wiped out the whole Israeli team at the Munich Olympics. And in our own backyard we had Basil D'Oliviera who could play cricket for England but not South Africa, the land of which he was a citizen. Just a second class one.

†††

I was always uneasy about the ills of South Africa being exclusively down to the race question. 'Working class' had a more substantial ring to it, it was beyond racism and apartheid as the cause of the problem, although it was clear that apartheid and South Africa were way beyond the pale.

Blacks were fighting for their rights in the USA, my contemporaries were objecting to Vietnam, Lyndon B Johnson and Richard Nixon didn't look a whole lot different to John Vorster. The world needed to change, and

I had hit on the idea that it was the working class that needed liberation from capital and capitalism as the solution to the problem. I had to learn the tools of such struggle, and they weren't to be found in South Africa. Marx, Lenin and Trotsky were waiting for people just like me in London. London was the answer, but I didn't have the means to get there.

My university studies were in disarray; I dropped out. My time living at home was over. I had had an argument over the supper table with my younger sister - the subject matter escapes me. My father ordered me to leave the table. The next morning he woke me, and berated me for my behaviour towards my sister. 'You have the manners of an artisan,' he said. 'That's exactly what I want to be,' was my reply. I have always felt a sense of discomfort over that remark, if only because I subsequently felt my father did not deserve that rejection of himself and his values, given the life that he had led. But it did signal that I was through with home and the family and had to move on. And my father sure as hell was not going to help me. So I went to live in Cape Town, to make enough money to get out of the place.

The 'orange people' cult had already been under investigation by district attorney Charles Turner for what he described as the 'largest recorded marriage fraud' in the US, in which 400 members took other cultists as spouses to evade immigration laws. In 1985, the cult allegedly formed a squad which included South African born Ann Phyllis Janks nee McCarthy of Fairwood Johannesburg. They bought illegal weapons and staked out Turners house, believing that by assassinating him the investigation would be derailed. The hit never took place, but Rajneesh was given a suspended sentence for the marriage fraud.

After the assassination failure, the cult started to unravel and several members confessed to federal investigators. South African cultist McCarthy was indicted for conspiracy to murder Attorney General Turner. In 1989, the FBI was brought in because McCarthy moved to Germany, married, changed her name to Janks, acquired joint SA-German citizenship and fled back to South Africa. She set up shop as an educational psychologist and did well. But the Americans continued to seek her extradition.

In December 2002 Phyllis McCarthy pled guilty to conspiracy to murder and sentenced to one year in jail and a fine of $10,000. She was 4th in command of Rajneeshpurnam, she had been known as Ma yoga Vidya. Turner called her sentence laughable. In court statements McCarthy stated 'I cannot forgive myself for not being tougher at the time' and called her time with the group 'psychological torture'.

†††

Bob Dylan : Masters of War:
Come you masters of war…
You've thrown the worst fear, that can ever be hurled
Scared to bring children, into the world
And threatening my baby unborn and um-named
You ain't worth the blood that runs in your veins
How much do I know? How to talk out of turn?
You might say I'm young, you might say I'm unlearned
But the one thing I know, I'm younger than you
And even Jesus would not forgive what you do.
Let me ask you one question, is your money that good?
Would it buy you forgiveness, do you think that it could?
I think you will find, when your death takes its toll
On the money you've made will never buy back your soul.
And I hope that you die, and your death will come soon
I'll follow your casket on a pale afternoon,
I'll watch while you're lowered, down to your deathbed
And I'll stand by your grave to make sure that you're dead.

†††

John Lennon: 'Working Class Hero':
As soon as you're born, they make you feel small
By giving you no time instead of it all.
Till the pain is so big you feel nothing at all
A working class hero is something to be
They hurt you at home and they hit you at school
They hate you if you clever and they despise a fool
Till you so fucking crazy you can't follow their rules
A working class hero is something to be

When they tortured and scared you for twenty odd years
Then they expect you to pick a career
When you can't really function you're so full of fear
A working class hero is something to be
And you think you so clever and classless and free
But you're still fucking peasants as far as I can see.
A working class hero is something to be
There's room at the top they're telling you still
But first you must learn how to smile as you kill
If you want to be like the folks on the hill
A working class hero is something to be
If you want to be hero well just follow me

Durban Southbeach 1969.
Haynes, Berman(RIP), Hoddes,
Levy – taken by Scottys.

Terence, Mum, Dad, Tim (Author)... circa 1957, Marina Beach, Natal.

Tim Haynes, 1954 long before the wheels actually came off.

KES – first team rugby, the author without a badge not really one of 'the boys'.

HEAD BOY, PREFECTS LOSE RANK AFTER RAID

Express Reporter

ALL except two of the prefects at the King Edward VII High School in Houghton, Johannesburg, handed in their badges in sympathy with four of the school's prefects, including the head boy, who were demoted after two alleged raids on a master's home.

The school's headmaster, Mr. H. R. Corbett, told a hushed assembly of the whole school on Friday morning that he had decided to strip the four prefects involved in the alleged incidents of their prefects' badges.

Two other boys, not prefects, who were also involved in the alleged incidents were to be caned. Mr. Corbett told the assembled boys that he had decided against a more severe punishment, because the teachers still had faith in the boys in spite of what they were alleged to have done.

The two raids — the second of which took place last weekend — were against the home of a senior master. It is alleged that the boys damaged a fence, dug up some flower beds and threw stones on the roof of the house.

Immediately after the assembly a group of the prefects handed in their badges to Mr. Corbett in sympathy with the prefects who had been demoted. However, the badges were later returned to them.

Among the prefects to have their badges taken away was the popular head prefect, Donald MacDonald. A keen sportsman and a member of the school's first rugby XV, Donald is well-liked by all the boys at King Edward.

The other demoted prefects — Timothy Haynes, Gavin Craig and Douglas Klerk — are also among the school's most outstanding sportsmen.

When I phoned Mr. Corbett he refused to make any comment.

I read the news today – Oh boy!
Head boy prefects lose rank after raid.

Protest meeting at Wits University on Jan Smuts Avenue – with Gil Brokensha, Tim Spiegel, Josh Heyman – 1972.

South African Voluntary Service – an organisation at South African Universities engaged in school building programs for African schools during the 1960s and 1970s.

David Dison, Clive Cope and Author mixing concrete with Max Debenge.

SAVS camps building sites, meetings & other social engagements.

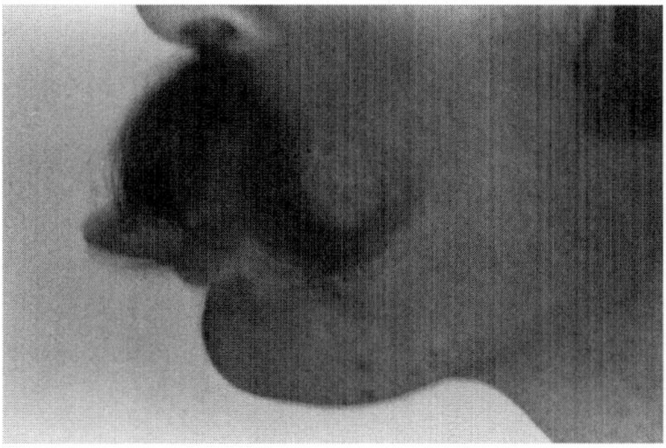

STORY 2

THE ARMY AND APARTHEID – A COMBO TO DIE FOR?

Athol Fugard said: 'I think it is under great desperation that ordinary things can happen in a human life. And if ever there was a country supplied with desperation it was South Africa at that time.'

†††

Gunner T.R.Haynes 69481471
By the authority of the State President of the
Republic of South Africa
You are instructed by the South African Defence Force.
To make yourself available for military duty
At Tempe Military Camp, Bloemfontein,
Republic of South Africa
On 4 January 1976 for a duration of
three months
This order may act as instruction to your employer, that
in terms of Act 345 (Part.2) 1974, you will remain in paid

***employment and paid in full in your absence
on military duty
This instruction may be used as transport pass to above
destination by any means FOC***

†††

I held the card in my hand, the nightmare card, just arrived in the mid-day post. There was no darkness to hide away in, no morning when the dreadful blackness would succumb to the morning light taking its horrors with it. I was caught, trapped by the brightly illuminated sentence.

Three months, three months' military service at Tempe. That was near Bloemfontein in the Orange Free State. The province where Apartheid decreed that Indian people could have passage through, but must not stop. Bloemfontein in army terms meant Angola. My mind was scrolling desperately: it couldn't happen to me… but, it just did. 'What if I left today…', got on a plane to London or walked across the border into Botswana and claimed refugee status? I didn't have a passport in order. Or money. This was puerile nonsense. I am an adult now, my parents cannot write a sick note. But my mind would not stop running, searching for a chink through which I could squeeze back to the freedom the card in my hand had just removed. Nothing came up. The blood had left my face, left my head. I felt faint. I felt cold and white. I could smirk at the irony. I was white, that was the problem here. Being white was a blessing in Apartheid South Africa. Now it was making me feel ill. And taking this latest development to its conclusive possibility, it might even kill me.

The truth was, I'd botched it. I had promised myself I would never do military service again, that I would leave the country before that day came. I could get an Irish passport, I had a brother living in London: it would be easy for me. The prospect of living in England, just out of the sixties, instead of in South African oppression depression, was not unattractive.

But the call had come earlier than I expected. I was caught, and it was too late to do anything about it.

The initial shock receded into frustration and anger at my predicament. It was time to start paying dues for that white privilege. But I've hardly started accruing the benefit to myself, I'm too young, it's not my fault I was born here, I snivelled to myself. I might have held the masters of Apartheid South Africa in contempt, and maybe not for the best of reasons either. Now I was off to defend their system, and them, and the white me, as Gunner TRHaynes.

†††

Several years earlier I'd done my original army service, followed up with another two military training camps. But this was of a different order. This wasn't a joke army anymore. This was to be guns with live bullets, in Angola. Everyone knew it was Angola because the politicians and the media were being evasive about South Africa going into Angola. Even Mr. J.B. Vorster (the prime minister) put it like this… 'First of all I cannot tell you how many South African troops are, let us say, actually on Angolan soil at this stage, and even if I knew, naturally I wouldn't tell you about it.'[1] After all, the rest of the world was unhappy about South Africa's presence even in the then South West Africa (now known as Namibia). The Apartheid regime was certainly not going to admit to being in Angola.

Adv. Vorster changed his tune to admit and justify involvement in Angola in a speech in the House of Assembly a short while later (Jan 1976). He said… 'We went in to chase Cuba and MPLA away from the dam… And I want to be candid with this, it is rather difficult. Sir, when you chase a man away to decide when to stop. That candidly is a difficulty. Naturally it must be left to the people who are responsible for doing the job to decide how far they are going to chase away the man, knowing that if they chase him away a short distance he may come back. I make no bones about the fact that we chased him a very long way.' That was how he spoke, he had a way with words. And that was how he was, South Africa's iron man at the top.

Gunner TRHaynes was now off to help chase away 'the man'. Or to put it another way, to protect the fatherland from the domino effect of communist victory in Angola, followed by communist victory in South West Africa, followed by communist victory in South Africa. These were some of the coldest and most desperate of Cold War days.

The following day I was meeting my friend Roy at Newlands cricket ground, Transvaal against Western Province in the Currie Cup. The day was bright, the ground was green, the white picket fencing around the ground looked like the tracks of the railway that would soon be ferrying me off to the army. Devil's Peak, the back of Table Mountain, was its usual breathtaking self. But I felt like a man with a sentence hanging over his head. I told Roy my news. He looked glum. We lay on the grass bank in silence. The players came out in their dazzling white. I put on my shades. The opening bat was Wynand van der Aardt. I recognized the name. I lifted the binoculars and recognized the face. I had been at the same school. I wanted to tell him I was going to Angola. He was a big shot, he would have some good advice. Roy passed me a cold beer and we settled down to watch Wynand.

Wynand van der Aardt, opening bat, got ten, although he hung around the crease for some time. He was devoid of technique and style. How could they select someone so inept? He was the same at school, confident but having no substance. Some things just never change. I was bitter. I was depressed. I asked Roy what I should do. He said I probably had to go. My mood slid far into the gloom, the clickety-clack torment of the troop train the only sound in my metronome darkness, counting down the days.

†††

The first line of the card rang through my head. Gunner TRHaynes. Gunner suggested the idea that a gun was involved, but I'd never really fired a gun in my life. During my initial army training I had hung a gun on two little hooks above my perfectly squared off bed. On the front of a shelf sat my kit bag, with all the pouches filled with wads of paper to square off the shapes of the pockets and ensure that they sat at right angles to the shelf. Those squared off pocket shapes gave the impression of disciplined soldiering. Once I'd not adequately cleaned the rifle before an inspection. The corporal had looked down the barrel into the light, had told me he could see an elephant in there and told me I should take another look at it. As I did so, he hit me with his rifle butt on the back sending my eye into the barrel of the gun. While that was quite a laugh for the other gunners and the corporal, my sore eye did not contribute to improved shooting skills or military discipline.

There was another reason I and the gun never really got close. My initial military service was in Cape Town, Youngsfield Military Base. I was eighteen, leaving home in Johannesburg for the first time. My mum didn't cry, she wasn't the crying type. Neither did I, there didn't seem any point. Together with five hundred others we struggled under impractical bags and suitcases onto the troop train. The base in Cape Town, the furthest point in South Africa from any border, was the home to anti-aircraft defense in South Africa. Maybe the masters of Apartheid thought that Cape Town would be the last peninsula to defend. The term 'Gunner', was used to describe the guy who sat on one of those gun and seat combos, rotating, bobbing and weaving all at the same time, and leaving a puff of exploded white smoke high up in the sky, usually long after the plane had gone. The motion of the gun was now guided by a radar system housed in a large mobile container sited close to the gun. The 'gunner' had no ability to determine where the gun would rotate and point to next. It was much like riding an octopus at the town fair. You just spun round and round, up and down. What was the point of the 'gunner'? This Gunner never got near this kind of gun either, so whether there was a point or not was debatable.

Gunner TRHaynes did his initial military service in 1971, a year which was to commemorate ten years since the declaration of the Republic of South Africa. There was to be a huge military display to mark the occasion in Cape Town. These decades were all about big military displays worldwide. The Soviet and Eastern Block displays were legendary and scary. They are out of fashion these days, except in North Korea. The South African display was also meant to be scary, not only to other African countries but especially to the vast majority of the indigenous population who were second class citizens, excluded from anything and everything by Apartheid.

Practice for the show was in full swing with even the air-force and navy involved. Three Mercurius jet fighter planes got lost on a cloudy day in Cape Town and flew into Table Mountain just above the Rhodes memorial. We were on parade at Ysterplaat at that moment and heard the noise. A friend of mine in the air force was sent up there on guard duty, until they'd cleaned up the mess. He said it was quite eerie being there through the night with bits of meat hanging in the trees. And this was peace time Cape Town. The war, internal or external, hadn't even started yet.

Our intake were trained as drivers, not gunners, to drive the trucks in that vast column of military weaponry from big guns to ready-to-unfold kitchen units. We learnt to drive the British Bedfords and the big German Magirus Deutz up and down the streets of Cape Town and over the dunes of Kraaifontein and Strandfontein, taking turns at it while the instructing corporal slept in the passenger seat and another seven gunners-cum-drivers slept in the back of the vehicles.

At the Youngsfield Military Camp, it was a case of surviving the army as best one could. The whole trick, the whole point, if one was of a certain mental disposition, and I was, was to ensure that one was involved in as little as possible. Whatever gap one could take to avoid an activity had to be taken on principle. After all Prime Minister John Balthazar Vorster was infinitely more scary than one's own parents, Apartheid was (even for a naïve white adolescent) not an attractive system, and the army was an accepted part of growing up as a prepared, capable and disciplined citizen. Some few brave-hearts were growing conscientious objection, but it was yet to become a viable option. Back in 1971, one's objection was registered by apathy, the art was to stop just short of indiscipline.

†††

Soon after arrival at the Youngsfield Military Camp for my initial army service, the new intake was assembled on parade and the Jews were ordered to make themselves known. A number of my friends from Johannesburg stepped forward. There was Barry Levy, Howard Isarow, Adrian Jaspan (who not so much stepped as limped forward as he had already been struck down with a debilitating attack of flat feet). I was left behind in the ranks crunched between some huge Afrikaners from places like Calvinia and De Aar. My Jewish friends beckoned to me that I should come with them, this wasn't to be the holocaust, this was to be getting out of camp on a Friday night and maybe even a Saturday morning to go to shul. In addition, being a Jew meant not having to go to church parade and church on a Sunday. Being a Jew meant eating from the kosher kitchen, where superior food was cooked by Jews who could at least be trusted not to piss in it for fun as would happen in the main kitchen. I thought instantly of these advantages, I took a deep breath, and stepped forward into the ranks of the Jews. I found myself standing next to someone else I was at school with. Robin Hancock was his name and he looked about as Jewish as Archbishop Runcie, the then man at Canterbury.

'Jeez,' I whispered to him, 'I never knew you were Jewish.'.

'My mother is Jewish,' he said, 'and although you probably wouldn't know it Haynes, that's important in the Jewish faith.'.

'I didn't, but I do now,' I replied.

That Friday night I got on the military bus that was ferrying all us Jewish servicemen up to the synagogue in Newlands. I was supported by my genuine Jewish mates who were explaining to the rest of the twenty five or so strong community that my mother was Jewish.

We arrived at the shul. All of the regular Jewish lads from Cape Town were welcomed by their parents and families, happy to meet for the first time since basic military training had begun. Each of the Jews from outside the mother city, with no welcoming family or friend to speak of, was allocated a host family. I found myself introduced to the Schers, a well to do Cape Town barrister, his immaculate little wife, their immaculate blonde tiny daughter, and family to Benjy, their soldier boy, a dumpling with pink rosy cheeks and thick gold rimmed glasses. Both Benjy and the Schers were happy to do their Jewish civic duty and look after me, I was very happy to make such accommodating acquaintances, even if it was fraudulent. Finding an ally, a friend, a bit of support for their vulnerable looking son in the hostile environment of an army camp was a small comfort to them.

Mrs. Scher zeroed in on me immediately, firing questions as to my family and its Jewish history or at least connection. I was stammering and stuttering, a glib statement about a Jewish mother might satisfy some defence force halfwit, but it certainly wasn't going to be good enough for Mrs.Scher of the Newlands Reformed Congregation. I was saved by the bell and we all trooped into the service. I nodded and bowed in imitation of the guy next to me, kept my eyes on the book, generally crapping myself about how long I might be able to pull off this deception. The army was one thing but how was Mrs. Scher going to react when she discovered I was just a smart-arse Jo'burg yok. She and her interrogations, which I knew had not even begun in earnest, were totally scary. I spent the entire service in prayer, requesting help with the interrogations that lay ahead, and fully realizing that there was no chance in hell my prayers would be answered. At the end of the service I caught my friend Barry held up in the queue leaving the synagogue, whose mother was just like Mrs. Scher. I hoped he might have some sage advice on how I should handle the evening still ahead with the Scher family.

'You got me into this mess, now how am I to withstand this interrogation the whole night long,' I asked him.

'Just tell her your mother's Jewish,' he said, grinning.

'Oh fuck off,' I said, right there in the synagogue, no doubt undoing any good work my presence and the nodding might have accomplished.

'If I remember correctly, from our days long ago at school together, in the swimming pool change rooms you once showed us your circumsized nob,' said Barry, laughing again, 'as a last resort, why not show it to Mrs. Scher?'.

'Good idea,' I said, 'and goodbye'.

The Schers were waiting for me on the steps outside. They said their goodbyes to their community friends and we found Mr Scher's black Jaguar which glided us back to their chic apartment on the top floor of a very upmarket Newlands block. Mrs.Scher kept up a pleasant chatter about the gossip she'd picked up in shul, who was there, who was wearing what, and who had said what about who was there and what they were wearing. And Mrs. Cohen's nephew Aaron was down from Johannesburg, did I know them, because everyone knew the Cohens in Victory Park. No, I lived in Observatory, I said, the other side of town. And the subtle little probing had started.

We sat down for the traditional Friday night meal. While the Schers weren't orthodox religious, they did the basics when it came to the prayers, the readings, the blessings, the candles, the food, the wine, the Ameins, the bowing. And every time something had to be said or something to be broken or dipped, Mrs. Scher's beautifully made up eye was on me like a hawk, and when I was particularly late on imitating soldier Benjy's Jewish moves, she picked up my hesitation and gave me a little wink. Then her probing stopped forthwith, and whenever she did mention something particularly Jewish again she made a point of catching my eye and giving me another of those little winks. She'd obviously made up her mind on the weakness of my Jewish credentials, but fortunately she'd simultaneously decided pragmatically that even a suspect Jew could do no harm as an ally for her son Benjy in the armed forces.

Each time I caught her winking eye, I gave a little smile which was only good manners, but was now also a kind of admission of guilt. The smiles slowly became smirks as the winking continued and I started considering ways of trying to stop the wink. If I replied with a little wink of my own, me, an eighteen year old boykie, albeit with circumcised nob, yes that would definitely stop the wink, but could have other unfortunate consequences. It looked like I was in for the long haul on it. I just had to hope she didn't hate me by the end of it.

†††

Back at the military camp we were all surviving as best we could. I discovered being a Jew lowered me a further rung on the army social ladder. Obviously there were all the ranked individuals, fifteen in all from general right down to lance corporal who could bully a gunner with the full might of the South African state behind them. After that there were the social strata. The Afrikaners were one up on the English speakers, because of their superior motivation (they believed in the army stuff, the English's belief was suspect). They were the 'rockspiders', we were the 'soutpiele'. Then there were the 'ou manne' (old men), regular troops who had been serving six months longer than our intake who assisted with enforcing another discipline quite of their own making. Our intake were known as 'roufs' (scabs), and I was an English speaking Jewish rouf with no rank.

My being a Jewish rouf caught up with me in a most unpredictable way. One morning I was standing in the breakfast queue and was nearing the front when an 'ou man' pushed in front of me. I gave him a shove and told him to get to the back of the queue. We were all holding our army issue steel plate, knife, fork and spoon set. He ripped his set apart and stuck the knife, touching the skin, under my eye and said,

'Wat se jy?'(What did you say?).

'Niks' (Nothing)I said, in shock and horror.

'Ek het gehoor, jy het iets gêse?'(I heard you, you said something) he said, again. The queue had gone quiet, the gunners craning their necks to see what would happen next.

'Ek het niks gêse,'(I said nothing) I said again, beginning to shake.

He took the knife away from my eye but held it in front of my face.

'Jy's a 'clever boy' ne. En na ontbyt ek sal jou wys wie's clever.' (After breakfast we'll see who's clever) He said. As the queue slowly advanced into the mess he taunted me all the way, telling me to enjoy my breakfast as it was the last I would be enjoying in a while.

I sat with some mates over breakfast trying to persuade all, or at least one, to support me in some way. There was much sympathy but no takers. I looked for a way to sneak out of the mess I was in. The 'in' doors were now shut and bolted against late comers. The only set of 'out' doors opened onto the washing-up area beyond. I looked for someone in authority I might turn to, but only saw hostile faces looking forward to some after breakfast entertainment. I said the Lords Prayer under my breath, and then in my new, still broken Yiddish I asked HaShem to calm this violent idiot down and forget about it. I exited the mess into a waiting crowd of two hundred, in front of which was the man with his shirt off and fists up. It was like a bad old black and white American forces movie. I gave my still clean eating gear (I hadn't eaten anything), to a glum looking Jewish chum, and faced off against the chataysim. He was shorter than me but thick set. I knew nothing about fighting. I'd never actually had a fight in my life. I was never a confrontational type, I was the second born, my older bolder brother did the confrontation. I did it my way when no-one was looking. Now there was no other way.

He lunged forward, toeing me with his boot in the middle of my shin. But then he retreated. He obviously didn't want to take a punch if he could help it. The information that for all his masculinity he was also a little nervous, gave me some encouragement. I lunged forward with my fists. I missed him as he sprung backwards. But he tripped off the step from the washing area into the road. He was on the ground. His head was at boot height. My foot shot out spontaneously against the length of his face. He was below me now, I was down, my knee on his chest and clubbed his head with my fists. Left, right. Left, right. His arms came up but I clubbed them away. My nervousness and fear had evaporated. I was now overwhelmed by rage; now that I could, I wanted to punch this idiot face to a pulp. After a few more moments the crowd washed over, pulled us apart, he looking groggy, me the furious lunatic. Soon calming down, I thanked my returned atheistic stars that I was still alive. And that was that. Or so I thought.

The happiest chappy in the whole camp was my new friend Benjy Scher. I started hearing rumours that if anybody so much as looked at Benjy askance (and a lot of the wanna-be dogs-of- war did), he threatened that he had only to say the word and I would come and deal with them in the same way that I had dealt with the lunatic from the breakfast queue. It was now pay-back time. I had to start paying for that Jewish Friday night happy meal and weekend, and the price tag was looking excessive. Benjy Scher's right to swagger around the military camp was going to cost me a stoved in head sooner rather than later. Even fresh from my victory I was realist enough to know that it was based on an extreme piece of good fortune, one that no bookie would give good odds on being repeated. I had to tell Benjy that I wouldn't be coming to his rescue in the event of his running into trouble with the big chataysim back at camp.

Of course the moment I told Benjy I wouldn't be attempting to save his ass as a result of any reckless situation he might get himself into, I was kissing goodbye to Mrs.Scher, figuratively speaking of course. Her support of me, never based on any religious connection, would melt like a snowflake falling in the desert in Canaan. And then by extension, poof would go the support of the rest of the entire Jewish community down at the shul. I was, from then on, to be a lonely wandering Jew unable even to renege on my Judaism without being in even more trouble back at the military base. Rather get out of sight for a while like Moses, resign from the team, lie low, and see what happened. Even that strategy was flawed by the fact that I wasn't actually a Jew anyway.

†††

First up, I could no longer join my Jewish mates on the bus legitimately escaping the army camp on a Friday night. Like before the fight, all my Jewish chums were sympathetic but none of them were from Cape Town so they were once again not in a position to offer tangible support. And importantly, these Friday night outings had become weekend outings, because of the religious nature of the Jewish Saturday and the fact that the Jews were not eligible for church parade roll call on a Sunday. So whether I liked it or not I had to get out of camp on a Friday night at the same time as the Jewish bus, and not return until Sunday.

Youngsfield Military Base had an airfield, and all the anti-aircraft hardware was stored in hangars along its strip. The airfield ended in a bog close to the main road going into Wynberg, Cape Town. This edge of the camp was not enclosed by heavy fencing, just a few strands of barbed wire. Donning vest, running shorts and tackies, and having filled a small tog bag with some civilian clothing, I set off as if I was doing an early evening jog. I plodded my way through the bog, between the strands of wire and proceeded up Wetton Road into the suburbs of Cape Town. Cape Town was a strange city to me. I knew nothing of its geography, or the very little that could be seen from the front of a Bedford truck I was learning to drive. I saw a sign saying 'Muizenberg', which I knew to be the beach. I hitched a ride in that direction.

The very first vehicle that stopped was a Morris Minor 1000, a legend of a car even though it wasn't yet dead. It was driven by a soldier; I could see his corporal's stripes through the window. My first thought was 'Military Police'. I'd been bust not 10 metres from the fence. But Military Police and Morris Minor 1000 were not a credible mix. I approached the car gingerly.

'Get in,' urged the driver. I did, and he sped back into the rushing cars.

'I know you,' he said,' you went to my old school King Edward.'.

'Quite right,' I said, 'but I don't recognize you'.

He laughed. 'You wouldn't know me, I was in the boarding house for just four months before my parents moved down to Cape Town.'.

And so started a beautiful friendship. I stayed with Richard Harding in his log cabin at the back of his parents' house in Newlands. I went to the beaches with Richard, and he showed me how to surf. It was party time in Cape Town, with Richard's sister part of my new social set. I put a wig on my still fresh army shaved head which was an instant party hit. The next few months were a kaleidoscope of madness. Sneaking in and out of camp, wearing strange clothes, hiding in people's car boots, surfing with Richard, Richard's sister, smoked-out dope-induced never ending hazes. One day I was walking near his house and saw some coloured builders renovating a house. They beckoned me over in my army uniform. I went quaking a little, after all I was the thin white line, they were the enemy. They were passing round amongst themselves a smoking wad the size and shape of the recently completed Hillbrow Tower. They passed it to me. Given the situation I felt duty bound not to refuse their hospitality. I remember opening my mouth and placing my stretched lips around the soggy mess on fire at the other end, and sucking deeply. There were cheers, there was some clapping, somebody said 'tsay' in a high pitched voice. The Hillbrow Tower circulated around the builders, landed back on me, but I couldn't hear properly. Another round of sucking, my eyesight faded and then there was silence.

I woke up, it was pitch dark, it was quiet, I had been propped up against the wall of the house and left, there was no-one around. My 'step-out' gear was still on. I remembered I was in Cape Town in the shadow of the mountain, in the army, slowly the pieces of my life fell back into a vague whole like a puzzle, but with the mandatory few pieces that are always missing. Shit, I thought… that was some stuff.

And then it was all over, the army service, the army training. What happened? Where'd it gone? I had no idea. It was a space in time with no content. A blank. If my life was a sentence, it now had a long hyphen at the end of it. And I was back in Jo'burg, there was still no conversation or question, it was just the army. No one was interested in the newly trained soldier, now expected to think of the rest of his life.

†††

Some years later I returned to Cape Town and lived in MacBrides Lane, Harfield Village, Claremont. It's very white chintzy now. Not then.

Macbrides Lane entrance was between two dark and dingy shops, just a single lane (who the hell was Macbride?), just wider than the classic skyblue VW kombi which I carefully guided down the road. The terraced row of houses on either side were announced by a low wall enclosing the front stoep virtually on the kerb. At the end of the row there was an open lot inhabited by a car wreck, an Austin A30 from circa 1958. The Austin was home to an indigent named Wally, and opposite the empty lot was a terraced row of three houses that had been cheaply renovated. The first was the one I was to rent. Being desperate I moved in straight away. Not being conversant with the geography or demographics of Cape Town, I was not aware that this was an area in transition. Harfield Village had been a 'coloured area'. Apartheid dictated that the coloureds were to move to Atlantis, a new area somewhere out on the sands of the Cape

Flats, and whites were being moved into Harfield Village. Coming from Johannesburg I was aware of the big dramatic actions, the grand plans of Apartheid. The expulsion of blacks from Sophiatown, the high-profile demolition of houses and their replacement with Triomf was one of those. This was not the same, it was insidious, the slow attritional movement of people, one house at a time, no fanfare, nothing in the press, just grinding people out of their traditional areas and onto the dusty beach that was the Cape Flats, the new areas like Mitchell's Plain and Atlantis, well away from the expanding white hub of Cape Town.

The people themselves said nothing of this process. Being such a small and intimate road, I immediately came to know the indigent Wally, who spent much time at my kitchen table having some tea and attempting to park off under my roof if possible. It wasn't long before, through Wally, I knew everybody and everything that moved in the road on a daily basis.

There was the Benjamin family. I never got to know the beginning or end of it. The core of the family numbered fifteen. Mrs. Benjamin, matriarch, her face round, all smile lines, her body rotund, her chest ample, enough for everybody. The austere, all encompassing black long top coat covering pants underneath and finished at the bottom with a practical pair of polished black shoes and at the top a black doek thing that hung down her back was completely at odds with the personality of Mrs. Benjamin, who was altogether more jovial. (The word 'muslim' was not yet in the English language, especially for a white kid from Jo'burg). Within the orbit of the matriarch mum were the kids and men. All slight as sticks, the kids buzzed around like excited mosquitoes – the girls in service of the mum, the boys finding any amusement with which to pass the time. The men, sitting on the floor, legs crossed, discussed serious issues.

Salim was a boy of about five, the leader of a gang of just more than toddlers in the road. My photographs record eight of them. I asked Salim to draw a picture of his home. He drew a box with a triangular lid on it – the house. It had a chimney and a flower in the front of it, although neither existed in reality. The box house was empty – except for a large TV with rabbit ears aerial in the corner. In reality the house was full, full to the brim – but for some reason Salim only saw the TV, which at the end of each day's programmes would conclude with 'Die Stem' – the national anthem. Well, the white national anthem in Afrikaans, it wasn't really for the coloured Benjamins, but they could just get a look in.

†††

Most Sundays in Apartheid South Africa were desperately boring and appallingly oppressive. Nothing was allowed to happen. It was the Dutch Reformed church for the believers, and if one came from a secular family it was a sleep in the afternoon or visiting the relatives. Nothing was open, no shops, no movies, only the odd Portuguese café with a greasy pin-ball machine, which usually tilted easily and never gave a free game. And if one ventured out into the streets one could be treated to a violent assault by the South African Police on some poor black whose pass book was not in order. My parents employed a woman who cleaned the house and cooked, and a man who tended the garden. Darius was his name. He never wanted to worry my parents with his pass-book, so he always asked me to sign it. Me, a fifteen year old white kid, signing permission for a grown man to live in our white area. Even then I felt uncomfortable about it.

I took the kids from Macbrides Lane to the beach one Sunday. I didn't even know whose they were. I just announced we were going to the beach and eight kids jumped into my Kombi. I had to eject one who still had a nappy on and was sucking on a dummy with dried snot over the rest of its face. I couldn't deal with that. When all were packed onto the seats I told Salim to tell Mrs. Benjamin we were heading for the beach. She emerged from the house, waved pleasantly goodbye, without really noting the child content of the van. She appeared to trust me with this precious cargo even though we'd only just met and I was part of the tribe that was busy removing her and her like from their ancestral homes.

I thought taking a bus-load of non-white kids to exclusive white Clifton beach would be a bit too risky. I was prepared to gamble on getting a klap myself from some white bigot, but I didn't want to put the kids in jeopardy. After all it was just a day at the beach, it wasn't designed to be a grand political statement or provocation.

So we passed Clifton by, and half way to Llandudno beach, stopped at a quiet cove that had some beach and some boulders and few other people. The kids went wild. They probably didn't see much of the environment beyond Macbrides lane, and this place had it all. Eight small kids letting rip, the boys splashing each other in the water, throwing sand and stones and fighting, the girls collecting shells, making things in the sand, going off on little missions of discovery. Came the end of the day, everybody burnt, tired, and full of sand and salt, and Salim got stuck up a tree. He had advanced too far along an overhanging branch, couldn't advance further and with the bough bending ominously, he was too scared to crawl backwards. So he was stuck, paralyzed with fear. Up to that point I hadn't noticed any racial problem. Obviously I was too insensitive, but now with Salim up the tree the few other beachcombers who were also packing up to leave began expressing opinions on our party.

'Wat maak jy met daardie hotties op die strand?' said one.

'Who do you think you are bringing these coloureds to our beach.' said another.

And of course the classic…

'Fok daardie Hottentot, laat hom val, dan is daar een minder'.

With some prodding, poking and encouragement we got Salim out of the tree, and our party left the exclusive white western seaboard for the squalor but comfort of Harfield Village on the east side of the mountain.

†††

I was an unwitting pioneer of Apartheid in Harfield Village in that I had rented a house that had been cleared of its non-white occupants. It had been partially tarted up and rented on to whites. Unwitting in the sense that I was a Jo'burg boykie and had no idea of the immediate past history of the place. There were two other pioneers like myself in our terraced block. Next door to me was a young salesman surfer. And the third house was occupied by what at first I classified as white trash. Hennie was all burnt brown leathery skin, thin, tall and rarely seen out of a pair of khaki short pants with the pockets, the zip fly and button half belt. No shirt or shoes. Always with some alcohol nearby, a beer can in hand, a brandy glass not far away. One of those people who is always busy, tinkering away at something but also didn't appear to have a job. His wife Maybelle (I assumed his wife, they were older than me) was a sweet-looking nurse, round, neat, light skinned, dark haired; even the first time I saw her I wondered how she could possibly be teamed up with Hennie. I was about to learn another lesson.

Regularly there was some kind of altercation between Hennie and Maybelle: shouting and screaming, the closed curtains and doors could not contain the violence. It seemed Hennie was mostly drunk. On a bad night, stuff inside would be thrown or toppled and the crash of breakage would clatter down the road. One waited for the sound of someone finally falling, the thud of a body as they were either too exhausted to continue or had fallen down dead drunk. And that would be it until a few nights later.

Irrespective of what the night's activity consisted, the following morning one would hear through the shutters the footsteps of neat and tidy Maybelle walking down the Lane to work her nurses shift.

My meetings with Hennie in the street were about excuses. 'Hey Tim, join me for a quick toot,' he would slur at me from across the road. 'I'm busy at the moment but I'll see you later'. I didn't want to let him think I didn't want to. I started bumping into Maybelle with some consistency. It all started with my seeing her walking home from the near by railway station. I stopped to offer a lift. Then when I was leaving the Lane in the Kombi, she would appear and I would give her lift to here or there. She was quiet, reserved, she didn't want to divulge too much about herself. We'd end up talking about her nursing. She was spunky, attractive. She made a point of telling me she was not married to Hennie. I asked her what she was doing with him. She said they had a history, but didn't elaborate.

I returned from an outing late one Sunday afternoon to be greeted by a commotion in the lane. It was centred on Hennie and Maybelle's house. 'He's got a knife,' someone told me. It was the usual in the house, screaming and swearing, breaking objects. Neighbourhood folk on the street were unwilling to get involved, one reason I perceived was that these were not 'their people', they were white. The extended implication being that they were 'my people', and that if anybody should do something about this, it should be me. I saw Mrs. Benjamin in amongst the people. I went over to her.

'Has anyone called the police?' I asked.

'It's not as simple as that,' she said.

'What's the problem?' I said.

'If the cops come, most likely Maybelle will take the punishment.'.

'How's that? A drunk knife wielding lunatic and… she'll take the rap?' I asked.

'You guys create it, and then you can't even see it,' she said. 'Sy's a kleurling, she's a Hottie… playing for white, so if the cops walk in on this scene, the new better life she's trying to create for herself is bust before its even begun. Can't you see that?'.

At which point Hennie came flying out the door, naked but for his khaki shorts, looking more manic and blotto than his usual self. The manic aspect was given panache by the kitchen carving knife he carried in the hand, which had been used, for there was blood on it, on his pants and on his body. No sound came from inside the flat.

'I'm gonna kill that fucking bitch,' he shouted.

Probably under the weight of pressure from Mrs Benjamin's opinions and beady eye I felt I should intervene.

'Hey Hennie, what's up man?' I said, approaching him nervously. He was distracted.

'I'm gonna kill that fuckin bitch,' he shouted at me again, slurring and slobbering.

'What happened to that toot we were going to have?' I asked him.

'I'm busy, man, can't you see I'm busy,' he said, but calmer.

'You don't want to go to jail hey Hennie?' I said.

'I don't care, I just wanna kill...' he said.

'Hey it's not worth it man... for that bitch, jail. Nah, Hennie... c'mon.' I said.

'What?' he said, now confused.

'To go to jail, not worth it man. What for? Can't even get any fucking toot in there man. Not worth it.'

'She's such a fucking shit bitch,' he said, but he was now explaining to me the detail of the thing, he was losing impetus.

'Don't worry about her,' I said. 'Think about yourself, for a change. Get clever. Worry about yourself. The cops will be here any minute. They'll see the knife. Here just put that knife down before they see that. They don't want to see that man. Get clever. Put that knife down. Think about yourself.'

He thought about it. He was having a battle with himself but he put the knife down on the wall of the stoep. He was confused, he didn't know what to do now. He was looking at me, looking at the door.

'Get some dop, where's that toot we were going to have,' I said, thinking the only way to end this scene will be for him to pass out drunk, which couldn't be all that far away. Of course I didn't know what was inside. Where did the blood come from? Was she still alive?

There were a couple of old deck chairs on the stoep with us. I took his arm, he was suddenly looking tired, he allowed me to guide him.

'Here sit yourself down on this, I'll get us some dop,' I said. He slumped down into the canvas, no longer hyper, but dead tired. I took the knife went over to Mrs. Benjamin and said.

'I think he'll be asleep in a second, won't you check inside that she's okay.'

'She'll be okay for now, the slut,' said Mrs. Benjamin with contempt, 'her type will always be okay in the short term. But down the track… ' The unspoken message was clear… you play for white, this is what you get and it's what you deserve. You're certainly history in your community.

'Isn't that a little harsh,' I said, 'I mean she's only trying to make her life a little easier.'

'Yes, but if you take up with a poor white, with white rubbish, you leave your people behind and you become that rubbish. Then the day will come when this Apartheid thing is over, and we can make our way. We won't want to know her then, because we'll be going places and she'll still be poor white trash. Sy moet dink a bietjie further, the rubbish.'

Hennie was asleep in the canvas chair, Mrs. Benjamin turned on her heel, the incident of the day was over.

Monday carried on as per usual, there was no word on any injury to Maybelle.

Another week went by, and I happened to be home early from college (I was a part time student) on a Tuesday afternoon. I'd been home about half-an-hour when there was a knock on the door. I opened up and there stood Maybelle.

'Can I come in?' she said.

'Sure, sure,' I said. She appeared also to be straight from work. She was wearing a white nurse uniform even still with a little pair of scissors sticking out the top pocket. The frock was a touch too small, so the length was a touch too short, the fit was a touch too tight and the top two buttons were undone all creating an entirety which would not be out of place in some 'poesboek' as they used to say in the army.

'Thanks for what you did the other day, the man's mal, a maniac,' she said coming close.

'What are you doing with the lunatic?' I asked once again, knowing I wouldn't get the full answer if any at all.

'It's a long story… one that I can't really get into.'

'So what happens next Sunday when nobody's there to take the knife away?' I asked.

'No don't get me wrong, I hate the man and will get out of that situation as soon as possible, as soon as I can find a room in fact. Who do you share this house with?' she put her hand on my arm and then went another step further with… 'and I've seen no evidence of a girlfriend for you.'

She was suggesting, angling for something even more than tenancy. I represented the possibility of a step up on Hennie in the white world. If I had felt something other than sympathy for the woman, it might have been a challenge I would have wanted to overcome. But I hardly knew her. At best I liked her. Not enough to take on the Apartheid state and its consequences.

'Sorry Maybelle, I just can't help you.' I said. It sounded pathetic.

†††

I had a friend from Mozambique, Isabel Pestana, a Portuguese who was studying at Cape Town University. Her family remained in Lourenco Marques, just about to become Maputo. Portugal had departed its colonies of Angola and Mozambique and civil war was beginning to rage. Isabel was in a state of continual agitation and tension, biting her nails and chain smoking, not knowing what the day-to-day situation with her family was. And no inkling what their, or her fate might be in the future.

She phoned me one afternoon and said she couldn't talk, but could I help out some friends of hers with urgent accommodation, like tonight. She repeated that they were friends of hers, she needed this favor desperately and could I meet them at the station in half-an-hour. No problem I said. Don't be alarmed, they look a bit strange, she said.

I knew she was part of the radical Marxist student milieu in Maputo, so I was expecting to meet and harbour a few underground Che Guevara types, and that did make me a little nervous. After all at Witwatersrand University I had known Carlos Cardoso who spent much time being interviewed by BOSS (Bureau of State Security – security police). He was assassinated many years later, a journalist in Maputo, about to expose the corruption of the Frelimo elite in Mozambique.

At the appointed time I was at the Harfield road station, a train rolled in and when it rolled out two humans stood on the platform, with a rolled up sack between them. My car was parked in the road across the tracks and I couldn't get a proper look; they appeared to be wearing matching gear – they all appeared to be wearing a sack, that is them and the sack.

They emerged from the subway into the light. I was totally perplexed at this anamorphosis. They were indeed two human beings. But there all similarities ended. They were wearing hessian sacks from shoulder to near ground, no shoes. Both had long unkempt almost dreadlocks. One had a beard, I assumed the other was female. The middle sack had no hair or head, it encompassed the belongings. If these were a couple of Mozambiquan revolutionaries, their disguise was so radically chic, it could only be drawing more attention to themselves, not less.

I was feeling a little put out and angry, I thought I was being dragooned into assisting with the revolution, but this… I would be demanding an explanation from Isabel.

'Hello,' I said. The sacks each raised a hand in greeting, before lifting their sack into the back of the vehicle. When we were seated ready to take of I said 'my name is Tim.' I turned to them for some reply.

'Ve haf no names,' the man said.

'Oh,' I said wondering what new weird and wonderful sect had cast them out into the world, or maybe they were just busking on their own. If this was an idea they were putting out themselves, it was a big statement. But did it have the backing of anything solid I wondered. This was 1975, and as hippies and hippie-dom began to fade the desperadoes came out attempting to keep it alive by presenting stuff even more outlandish than had so far been on offer.

I drove the few blocks to the house with the sack people in silence. They followed me into the house. I showed them the floor in the living area where they could lay their stuff, went in search of something that could be used as a mattress and returned with a skimpy piece of foam. Oh no, no they gestured, and put their grass mat directly on the floor. I showed them where the lights and plugs were. Oh no, no they gestured… and pulled out a candle from their provisions. The thrust of the idea appeared to be back-to-basics; comfort through development and technology bad, hardship and old days/old ways good.

They weren't too interested in me, me being an ordinary boring not rich person. But as we passed somewhere in the house I did ask them what they were doing. It was a fairly open question which could have been interpreted in many ways. They answered it as follows:

'Ve are travellers.'

'And how do you travel?'

'In many vays, but mostly wif the feeet.' Well they had come in the train and my car in the last half hour, so this was another metaphysical answer.

'Ve came on a horse in Suid-Wes Africa,' he elaborated further.

'Is your family in South-West Africa?' I ventured, remembering the Germans there.

'Ve ver vonce valking in za desert, and ve saw a man coming tovards us. Ven he got closer, ve saw it wos our fazer,'

'Did your father know it was you?' I asked.

'Ja,'

'And what happened then?'

'We spent za night togezer, the next day we carry on.'

This wasn't going anywhere. It seemed like they had cobbled together an outrageous image and then were busking the rest on an anti-technology, mystic – voodoo ticket. These new religions were getting very sloppy. I got Isabel on the phone, and told her that she couldn't have both me and them as her friends. She had to choose. I felt unhappy when she said she preferred me, but left it at that.

I heard him shuffling down the passage.

'Vhere is the Garden of Eden?' he asked me.

'In Eden,' I replied. At least we were both now confused.

'No,' he said. 'I'm looking for za toilet space.'

'End of the passage,' I pointed.

He shuffled off down there but was back in a moment.

'No,' he said, 'is zere no garden space?'

'Straight out the back,' I directed once again.

He went into the garden and had a piss. Later that same night before going off to bed, they both went into the garden, dug a small hole, had a shit and covered it up.

The next day I awoke in a tetchy mood. My life was a mess, My housemates were dressing in sacks and shitting in the garden. I was living with a coloured woman next door slowly being murdered. I was about to go off to the army, probably Angola. Oi vey. Something… no, everything had to change. I resolved to book my ticket exiting South Africa the day the army camp was complete, and the sacks must go. I went off to work as per my regular programme, a day on the building site in the sun and the dust, and booked my ticket at lunch time. I arrived home and walked in as the one with the beard of the two sacks sidled over and turned off the radio which had obviously been their companion for the day. They wouldn't use the toilet but the radio was okay. I was finished with it. I said to the sack people, tomorrow you leave. I wanted no ambiguity, no misunderstanding, no mistake in translation. Okay he sang out as if he recognized a fair cop. The next morning they were gone. So was I four months later, after my army camp. South Africa and me were through, for the next eighteen years, until my return in 1994.

†††

Roy was right. He had told me at the cricket I probably had to go to the Army camp. As instructed I arrived for my appointment with the SADF in Bloemfontein, the transit camp for South West Africa (Namibia), and then of course, I immediately fell in with dubious company, the drinkers, the rookers, the passive resisters, in short those that kept under the radar for many and varied reasons. Existence in the army when one is not a 'believer', is like that of a condemned man or a recovering alcoholic – one day at a time. The days consisted of trying to hustle the best deal for oneself… where to find the best food in which kitchen at what time… where to get a shower… how to avoid any physical activity… who to avoid… who to keep on the right side of.

We'd stopped off in Grootfontein on the way to Rundu on the river border with Angola. Grootfontein was the main supply base for the whole South African involvement in Angola. The camp was in a state of massive and rapid expansion. New army divisions and their arms and equipment were arriving every day. The first serious South African incursions into Angola were about to take place, under the command of the soon to be famous Colonel Jan Breytenbach, brother of the soon to be famous Breyten Breytenbach. Jan for his initial successes in defence of the South African regime, and Breyten for his attempt to develop an organization to overthrow the South African regime. Both of them failed.

The sack people became quite an item in Cape Town for some years. She had a miscarriage and at some point died. After that he became a regular guy for a while and then disappeared into the ether of normal society, selling houses, somebody said.

My non-compliance was made easy by the fact that there was nothing to do. Our job was to guard the airstrip at Rundu, on the river border between Namibia and Angola, against attack from the air. After all, we were the anti-aircraft artillery and gunners. This was before the arrival of Russian MIGS on the side of the Cubans and MPLA in Angola. My job was literally to look at the sky on the screen in the radar room and report the movement of any hostile aircraft. There were none. Of course there were supply planes coming in from South Africa and the Lear jet of PW 'die groot crokodil 'Botha, the South African Minister of Defence, usually on a special assignment.

What was more interesting than the empty skies was what was happening in the camp. SWAPO prisoners were held there, sometimes made to sit out in the baking 42 degree sun. A squad of foreign mercenaries were based there, personally instructed by PW himself and then absent from the camp into Angola for 'special assignments'. And the odd pile of body bags ready for flight back to South Africa, back to surprised and distraught families. The press and government were still silent about the presence of South Africans in Angola.

On arrival, we were welcomed by the top brass. PW himself was first to say a few vacuous words in Afrikaans about doing our duty as South Africans. At least he was among friends, so we did not have to endure that famous finger pointing or threatening. Then it was left to the top brass to reinforce the message. More military platitudes. The last speaker from the podium informed us that legally we could refuse to enter the sovereign state of Angola, and that for the sake of expediency if anyone intended exercising that right, he should do so now by raising his arm. A rumble passed through the crowd, clearly looking, nay hoping that some idiot would have the bad sense to raise his arm. Nobody took up the invitation to refuse.

The days were so hot they were spent in a sweaty stupor. At night there were choices to be made. Did one get into the duck down British made military sleeping bag and sweat to within an inch of death by dehydration? Or lie on top of the camp bed catching any light zephyr of cool, while being feasted on by a mega air force of mosquitoes? I tried it one night this, the next night that. Either way it was unplayable. This hell was made slightly easier by the alcohol sold in the army bush 'pub' at five cents a tot, supply unlimited, every night. This meant that the nights were spent in a stupor of a different variety.

One day I was fortunate enough to break out of camp aboard a Magirus Deutz truck to fetch the early warning observers. While we were watching blank radar screens back at camp for hostile aircraft, what of those that got through the radar undetected by, say, flying too low? To prevent such possibility, our cunning masters of war had placed observation posts ten kilometers away from the camp. They were manned by two troepies, whose job it was to look at the sky all day, and report anything detected. These posts were dug into a piece of open veld or bush, and even on a platform built into the top of a tree in a forested area. Anywhere for a good view. The Magirus Deutz would deliver and fetch the unfortunate troops day in and day out. The massive truck tore through the bush, over the veld, even through fields of produce tended by Ovambo women, who looked up from their work with an expression of complete non-comprehension, of incredulity and of course hatred at this violation.

The troops, overcome with boredom, blew their own minds with whatever they could lay their lips on, in this case local and very powerful marijuana supplied by the locals who did the really menial jobs in the camp. On this day we picked up Anton and Hennie who were still dazed from a heavy day imbibing and looking at the sky. Anton told me that that very day, he temporarily left the shelter to relieve himself of the beers that he had secreted away for their luncheon. He was swaying with happy alcohol and narcotic befuddle and became aware of a thick strand of bush swaying in time with him not two feet away. They swayed together until the long leak had diminished to a series of ever smaller splashes, at which point he realized that the swaying bush was actually a cobra as tall as he was. The 'early warning' job was a dangerous army assignment.

My three months in Rundu were marked by what must be considered to be a significant achievement by a soldier in wartime. I never killed anybody but I saved one person's life. It happened like this.

Each tent was home to six troops. Alongside myself was a gentleman named Eugene Olkers, from the south of Johannesburg, a no-hoper of monumental proportions both physical and mental. He was happy to be there in the army, on the border. He explained… no father to hit him, nothing to do, as much food as he could fit into his ample frame on as many plates as the kitchen tiffy's would serve him, and five cents for a tot of alcohol. And for these benefits he was required to do almost nothing at all. For Eugene, this was heaven.

At the end of every long evening in the bush pub, he would try to make his way back to the correct tent in the dark. Tripping over guy ropes, stumbling into canvas sometimes collapsing the whole thing to the ground, he occasionally made it back to the right tent before happily passing out wherever he lay. And on a rare occasion, he even made it to the right camp bed – next to me.

On one such rare evening he was lying so vrot drunk on his back, not even the mosquitoes were going there. Comatose as he was, he was gurgling like a baby. It was my night for inside the bag, with a tee-shirt over my protruding head. His gurgling went on for awhile, and then changed to a rattle like that of death. I realized that the gurgling was vomit welling up in his throat. In his passed out state, he couldn't move his head. He was drowning in his vomit. I lay there asking myself if I should save the life of this big bag of shit, whose life by his own description wasn't really worth living, or should I intervene, ensuring that he went back home to the South and lived hard and horrible. The devil in me got my arm out of the bag, stretched it across the gap between us, applied two fingers to his cheek and pushed his head over horizontally, allowing the vomit to come tumbling out of his mouth and throat. I had forgotten about the stink that would follow such a course of action. Eugene Olkers spluttered, coughed, spat back to life like an old Ford Cortina repaired by a backyard mechanic. I had saved the life of a fellow South African soldier.

And then it was all over. To say at the end that it had passed in a flash was nonsense. Every minute had been counted. It had felt like a lifetime, a waste of a lifetime, made worse by the fact that it was the last place on earth I had wanted to be. But it did make leaving the country to go to England something definite, not needing a second thought. In those dark days of 1977 it felt as though P W Botha and his power base were an immovable monolith, a monolith that would take many bodies to defeat if ever. In the event it took another seventeen years to arrive at the negotiating table and the final defeat of Apartheid.

1977 – farewell to South Africa party – with Mark Stein, Piers Cross, Sean Moroney, Nigel Penn, David Dison, Colin Mendelowits, Dave McKibbin.

Trying to take the army seriously at Youngsfield in CapeTown 1971.

Sean & Tim – McBrides Lane.

Harfierld Village 1976 with Wally's A30 home in the foreground.

McBrides Lane at night in 1976

Harfield Village night street scene taken in 1976 near McBrides Lane

Salim on my shoulders with other kids.

The Benjamin family in McBrides Lane in front of their home.

Benjamin family being moved out of MacBrides Lane for whites to move in. And still smiling.

Children in Manenberg Township - which was a state built and managed ghetto instituted by the Apartheid government. It was developed as a living area specifically for low-income mixed race families in the Cape Flats. The picture was taken 1972 near to Mitchel's Plane.

Chintsy Harfield Village in 2014… still not many black faces in sight?

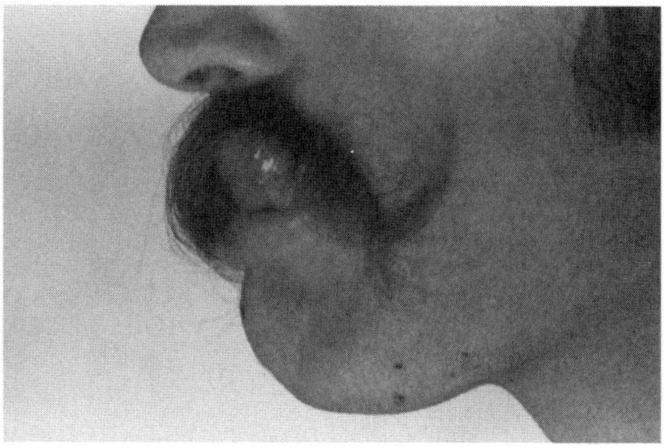

STORY 3

GENEALOGY: TO DO WHAT YOU HAVE TO DO!

If my life until my early twenties had been plotted on a graph, it would have shown deeper troughs and higher peaks than the tides of the Southern Ocean. I was unable to live life on an even keel. The highs were high, but to extricate myself from the lows took huge strategic thinking and effort. Why was that?

In my mid twenties I wanted to go off to the revolution. I was one of a minuscule minority who felt that way. Why were the rest not like me? I admit to having an inkling of what it might be, but I had tried to suppress it. It was not so much an issue hanging threateningly over my psyche, it was a part of the physical makeup of my body. Was it an illness? Did I need therapy? Drugs? Different drugs? How could I cut out the lows and stay up there on a high? Somebody said: 'Forget it mate, nothing you can do, it's in your genes.' At first I thought he said jeans, but no, it was genes.

So I'm talking genealogy, I'm talking my family, my roots, my genetic makeup, my DNA label, where I fit on the human supermarket shelf. How could I settle down to life anywhere as a 'normal' human away from a natural bent for lunacy if I had an inbuilt out of control mechanism? I got down to work on the family tree, being of the belief that I, as fruit, would not have fallen far from it.

†††

A woman named Letitia Haynes, another Haynes fruit, wrote a book called 'The Buried Past in Family History' published in 1993 in England. In it she documents our early family history, and I used this extremely informative publication to trace my origins. Of course she doesn't go as far back as the Cradle of Humankind or even Blombos; one would need DNA testing for that, but she does go as far back as our coming out of the Welsh forests into England. That was at the time of George III and the Napoleonic Wars.

Letitia Haynes wrote: 'It is recorded in family tradition that one of (the Haynes) forebears, Nathaniel by name, was sufficiently implicated in a political plot to get himself hung at Worcester gaol for treason. The exact nature of his offence has been lost in the passage of time but it was most likely connected with events during, or immediately after the Napoleonic wars, when social unrest greatly disturbed various governments of the day.'

I naturally wanted to check if she was right. The difficulty was that official records only became fully comprehensive in England after 1850. What I discovered in my investigation was that at the time (1793 to 1825) the law in England recognized 223 capital offences. These were attached to crimes of the slightest character. A person could be hung for appearing in disguise on a public road, cutting down young trees, shooting rabbits, poaching at night, picking pockets, stealing from a shop to the value of five shillings, from a private house, stealing a handkerchief from a private individual, being a gypsy and staying in one place for more than a year. Plus another 213 offences for which one could and would be 'hung by the neck until dead'. Public hanging was common, made private only in 1856. There were lesser punishments for lesser offences. Imprisonment for debt in England at the beginning of the 19th century meant imprisonment for life. If a person refused to plead in a criminal case, heavy weights, constantly increased, were placed on a person's body, and food refused him until he died. The unhappy recalcitrant usually took this course of refusal to plead, because if he did plead and was found guilty, the whole of his property would go to the king.

Fortunately for me and my genes quest, the words used to describe my ancestor Nathaniel Haynes' crime were 'implicated in a political plot'. The basis for the understanding of my own character and motivation would have been seriously undermined were Nathaniel hung for 'appearing in disguise on a public road' or for 'stealing a handkerchief from a private individual.' He would not have appeared in this book and the genealogy investigation would have been quietly dropped.

So Nathaniel was a good start to my quest. My second discovery was just as thrilling.

†††

My full name is Timothy Russell Haynes. I never got round to asking my own father why Timothy and where Russell. And then he was gone, his life suddenly cut short in a car accident. By the time I thought to ask my mother she suffered from Alzheimer's. I was left to research the question myself. I turned again to the family tree in search of a Timothy and a Russell.

There was one Timothy in my forebears. While still a youngster in 1860, this Timothy was kidnapped by 'bargees', a term for people who made a living transporting goods on Britain's network of rivers and canals. Timothy was kept by them for a long time travelling the canals of England, working with his captors on the barges. Eventually he escaped and got a job as a postman. Not much to get excited about there. But this Timothy's father was a fellow called Harry Russell – my great-great-grandfather.

Harry Russell was an Irishman from Dublin, and a committed member of the Fenians. The Fenians were an Irish nationalist organization dedicated to the liberation of Ireland through armed struggle. Harry had come from Dublin to Manchester when it was said 'things got too hot for him' at home in Ireland. In 1867 two Fenians – Thomas Kelly and Timothy Deasy – were arrested in the centre of Manchester. A week later they were conveyed from the courthouse in Manchester to the county gaol. They were handcuffed and locked in two separate compartments inside the police van with a posse of twelve mounted policemen to escort them.

On the journey, as the van passed under a railway arch a man darted into the middle of the road, pointed a pistol at the driver and called on him to stop. At the same time a party of thirty men leapt over a wall at the side of the road, surrounded the van and seized the horses, one of which was shot. The police being unarmed offered little resistance, and were soon put to flight. The rescuers, after a futile attempt to burst open the van with hatchets, sledge hammers and crowbars, called upon police Sergeant Brett, who was inside the van, to open up. He refused, whereupon one of the rescuers placed his revolver at the keyhole of the van and fired. At that moment the luckless Sergeant Brett had put his eye to the keyhole to see what was going on outside. Needless to say it was the last thing he ever saw. After a chase the police made 29 arrests. Five were sentenced to death, one was pardoned, one's sentence was commuted. Allen, Larkin and O'Brien were hanged on 23rd November 1867. They become known as 'The Manchester Martyrs'. Harry Russell was one of the Fenian 'rescuers'.

†††

Well, if I was looking for a revolutionary blood stream, I was on the right page in the map book. My investigation was throwing up the perfect evidence to prove my notion that I must contain some errant genes. And some evidence considerably less desirable which, for the sake of accurate scientific record, I must confess to … both Harry Russell and Richard Haynes, my two great great-grandfathers, abandoned their families and eloped with other women, never to be seen again. But I shall ignore this and stick by my thesis.

I was satisfied that I had enough of an account for the Timothy, the Russell and the Haynes blood coursing through my veins. The cherry on the top was next to come, in the shape of my own grandfather Harry Walter Haynes, who was born in 1884 in Birmingham, England, and died in Johannesburg in 1965.

Harry Walter Haynes was many things in his life, all of which he approached with a serious measure of rebellion. Fortunately, he could also list 'scholar and literary man' on his CV, so much of what he did, he also recorded.

'That I am a rebel; and always have been since I became old enough to think – I know, and I suspect that I shall remain one now until I go into the 'tongueless silence of the dreamless dust,' …he wrote in his later years.

Harry's family came from desperately poor circumstances, with no education to speak of. But his father, in spite of his illiteracy, built a rope manufacturing business in Birmingham and made good. Having made good, he insisted on quality education for his children. Young Harry assisted by winning a bursary to study at the prestigious King Edward VI public school also in Birmingham. Greek, French and Latin books filled his satchel. He was a star pupil but never pursued formal academia after school, as the rebel in him pointed in another direction. His first major act of rebellion came at age sixteen. He ran away from home, lied about his age and embarked on a troop ship bound for South Africa and the Boer War. He was desperate to escape the stifling socio-economic conditions of Victoria's England at the end of her very long reign.

†††

Seventy five years later I was a pupil at a King Edward VII School, but in King Edward VII School, Johannesburg, South Africa, modelled on and in fact a physical replica of the Birmingham original. Like my grandfather, each and every morning of assembly I gazed upon an enormous portrait of the later King Edward, a rotund ceremonial centrepiece.

My academic performance was less than satisfactory. 'Not performing to his potential' rang out one report-card after another, year after year for the full ten. Harry recorded his headmaster as writing on his report card, 'he is in danger of becoming a dull and uninteresting boy.' I pursued post school academia and failed at it; my interest in revolutionary politics got in the way of my University studies, and I ran away to England to pursue them more seriously. Harry had run away to war in South Africa before post school academia could even commence.

If school or parental authority could not contain Harry, neither could religion. From an early age Harry was unimpressed with the church, not because of boredom in which kids might normally be expected to express their objection, but with reflection. He wrote that the Church …'never seemed to have any relation to life. That has always been part of its beauty and its charm. It never seemed to have anything to do with me'… and 'I joined with two hundred odd other innocents to repeat in that cataract of words inseparable from the Psalms, Behold, I was shapen in wickedness, and in sin hath my mother conceived me, without astonishment, because quite obviously such words could not possibly relate to me'…

It was the same with me. Together with one thousand odd 'innocents' in my school hall, we were regularly encouraged, in that segment of early morning assembly given over to religion, to 'remove the log from our own eye before removing the splinter from that of our neighbour' – or some-such. Once again grandfather Harry explained it …'There seems in fact to be a lowest common denominator of sermons, the simple text, which has to be juggled with, as one juggles with vulgar fractions, until it comes to mean something quite different from what it seems to mean, and much more obscure.' So as with Harry, the purpose of church completely passed me by; religion had lost its power to dissuade rebellion or persuade compliance. Again Harry and I were on the same page.

At age sixteen, Harry Haynes surreptitiously boarded the troop ship headed for Port Natal in 1899, at the beginning of the Boer War. He was signed up as Major-General French's batman, probably on account of his capable horsemanship. The famous Major-General French as he then was, commanded the entire British cavalry force that came in through Durban, Natal to fight the Boers.

Harry's first boss was to become Field Marshal John Denton Pinkstone French, 1st Earl of Ypres, KP, GCB, OM, GCVO, KCMG, ADC, PC. He also became Lord Lieutenant of Ireland, just prior to Irish independence. A big shot.

French's first significant military assignment was to Egypt to relieve the besieged Sir Charles Gordon in Khartoum, Sudan. He (and 10,000 others) arrived two days late. Gordon had been killed, punctured by lance and beheaded. French was expert on horsemanship and the use of the lance and sword. That is old fashioned close combat. Anathema in today's world of war by distant remote. But the Boer War suited French's favoured fighting situation, for it was largely in broken country, much at close quarters on horse-back, where his expertise in the use of the various blades was especially useful.

He was a choleric little man, who tried to cover up his lack of height by always wearing an unusually long coat. It made him look shorter. Both the British military and political establishments had doubts about his intellectual capacity, which might go some way to explain why he finally got the top job in Ireland and why Ireland then won their war of independence from England on his watch.

Harry Haynes lived cheek by jowl with French, saddling his horses, polishing his shoes and no doubt shining those badges. They were together at the battle of Elandslaagte, followed by that at Lombard's Kop. French's British forces including Harry were trapped in the siege at Ladysmith but escaped, before French commanded the mounted forces at the Battle of Colesberg. After Colesberg a verse was published about him:

'E's so tough and terse.
'E don't want no blooming nurse.
And 'e ain't had one reverse.
'Ave yer, French?

†††

Next was the relief of the siege of Kimberley which French heroically secured with 8,000 cavalry men against 900 Boer defenders. The Battles of Paardeberg and Poplar Grove were en route to the capture of Bloemfontein and then Pretoria. In between these major battles, he was continually fighting off marauding Boer raiders or giving chase to eliminate them. For Harry Haynes this experience at such a young age must have been fascinating and instructive. He was doing what every young kid dreams of – except the blood and guts were real. Harry saw it all. And it was a complete introduction into the class system if ever there was one.

†††

Then it was 1902 and the war was over. Harry W Haynes, still a teenager, returned home to Birmingham. If Birmingham was stifling before his war-time experience, it now felt indescribably more oppressive. If Harry the boy soldier had arrived in South Africa a substantial sceptic of family, state and religious authority, there is no doubt that the military and politics would have been added to his list of detestations. South Africa had given him wide open spaces and freedom from a cold and controlled Britain. His father's rope manufacturing business was on its last legs, close to bankrupt. His father was old, ill and beyond pulling it back together. Harry reluctantly offered to do it, but it would have to be in his way. They fought. His father would not give in. It was just as Harry had foreseen. He once again packed his clothes, this time civilian, and took the next passage back to South Africa. He would only visit England twice more in his life. His father and mother (my great-grandparents) died shortly after Harry's leaving and in short space of each other.

On conclusion of the Boer War there was a huge drive from England to populate South Africa.

†††

Lord Milner, the British High commissioner for South Africa, wanted settlers for the Rand, the mines. Cecil John Rhodes, Prime Minister of the Cape Colony explained the British need: …'I was walking in the East End yesterday and attended an unemployed meeting. I listened to the wild speeches, which were just a cry for 'bread, bread,' and on my way home I pondered over the scene and I became more than ever convinced of the importance of imperialism. My cherished idea provides a solution for the social problem. In order to save the 40,000,000 inhabitants of the United Kingdom from a bloody civil war, we colonial statesmen must acquire new lands for settling the surplus population of this country, to provide new markets for the goods produced in our factories and mines. The empire, as I've always said, is a bread and butter question. If you want to avoid civil war, you must become an imperialist.' Harry Haynes and many of his English compatriots would not turn out to be quite what their British masters had in mind.

Back in South Africa, Harry needed a job. Relying on his horsemanship and his war experience, he joined the paramilitary colonial police forces. As exciting as this must have been, Harry's real interests lay elsewhere. The mining industry incorporated all that was attractive to him. The all-English underground aristocracy of labour not only brought their mining skills but also their trade union model which was well established and had proved successful back in England. He was in good company. The tin mining labour component from Cornwall had arrived en masse with the decimation of that industry back home. He became a miner and immediately started agitating for better working conditions, for trade union recognition, for political representation and power for the white mine workers. Words such as wage labour, surplus value, jingoism, syndicalism, class struggle started appearing in Harry's vocabulary. It was obvious who he was reading. He wrote of Guy Fawkes and the gunpowder plot of 1605 : …'the only man who ever went to parliament honestly intending to do something useful.'

With Harry's literary skills and his extrovert rebel nature he was immediately in the forefront of the leadership of these workers and their struggles. And there was his formative character driving him along: …'from early childhood I was trained to take the side of the weak. With me it is instinctive,' he said.

†††

Cut to the upstairs of the Grand Theatre in Benoni, June 1913. Benoni had become the heart of gold mining on the Witwatersrand. The Grand Theatre had become the centre of labour agitation. A strike committee was constituted and Harry Haynes was elected chairperson. All the heavyweights of the time were involved, Jimmy Bain, Tom Mathews, Bob Waterston, Archie Crawford, Bill Andrews, Walter Madeley and of course, probably the most radical of them all, Mary Fitzgerald.

The labour leadership was a powerful mix of experience and militancy, but the English industrialists were also experienced and ruthless. They were not going to be moved easily. Violent confrontation was to be the only outcome.

Jan Smuts, the Minister of Defence in Louis Botha's government, came to Benoni to resolve the strike. He failed. Smuts was ill equipped to deal with immigrant trade unionists. He loved the countryside, the quiet walks in intellectual thought and contemplation. He described Jo'burg as 'the Mecca of the hooligan'. In a sense Harry agreed with

Smuts ...'Johannesburg constitutes an independent free state in all but name. Here ordinary law cuts very little ice. The golden city is powerful enough to swing the whole country when it wants to, while the rest of the country remains impotent to swing Johannesburg. Every great wave of popular passion that rolls up from the back veld is quietly smothered when it strikes the soft sand of the Robinson deep dump.'

Smuts was a Cambridge educated lawyer used to the intellectual cut and thrust of politics in high places, with lords and prime ministers and powerful people, not English mine labour who sang the socialist anthem The Red Flag, threatened violence and were not intimidated by political power. The political radicals clearly had substantial influence among the miners. The whole affair was quintessentially English, but it was Benoni, on the South African Highveld, winter 1913. The soft sand of the deep dumps was ready to swallow another victim from the back veld.

The strikers upped the stakes with stone throwing, overturning vehicles and burning, the police responded with mounted and foot officers. In long frock and hair 'up', Mary Fitzgerald led her flag-waving women in support of the strikers, ratcheting tension still further. Smuts, realizing his impotence, then appealed for assistance from the British commander in South Africa who brought in the Royal Scots Fusiliers. Now the British forces were to fight British miners, at the request of the 'Boers'. A complete volte-face in the short years since the Jameson Raid and the Boer War. The convoluted nature of the relationship between Boer and Briton, English and Afrikaans, capital and labour, and then between English and Afrikaans capital which began with Rhodes and Jameson was now in full swing, elements of which remained until the end of white rule and arguably elements of which still remain today.

Sixty three mines had struck and the strikers called a mass meeting at Johannesburg's Market Square to inaugurate the general strike. A group of 10,000 people were assembled there, facing two squadrons of the Royal Dragoons, foot police and mounted police with long batons, to be told that Smuts had banned the meeting. Fist fights broke out; from nearby roof tops bottles and missiles rained down, the Royal Dragoons were ordered to draw their swords and cantered across the square lashing people with their flat blades. The crowd marched off through the city with intention to close Village Reef mine when Mary Fitzgerald appeared on Market Square, re-igniting the crowd and leading them to the power station in Newtown where they swarmed through the building and shut off the power.

As was usual in colonial mining towns, and especially in the 'Mecca of the hooligan', many of the assembled carried revolvers. White and black poor, and thugs now joined the melee for loot. The Johannesburg station was set alight. The Star newspaper offices were dynamited (the strikers regarded the Star as the mine owners' mouthpiece). The miners arrived at the Corner House, the head offices of the most important mining groups, but the armed forces had prepared themselves in anticipation of this. Now barricades were set up and there was exchange of gunfire. Smuts and Botha had lost control of the country's biggest city, and production in the land's most vital industry was at a standstill.

The following day the strike committee received a message that Prime Minister Louis Botha and Jan Smuts had arrived from Pretoria and were now in the Carlton Hotel, willing to open immediate negotiations. Strike committee representatives Bain, Mathews, Waterston and a union official called Hindman were soon on their way to the Carlton.

While battles continued between police and those at the barricades, finally a deal was hammered out by the two parties. The concessions of Botha and Smuts do not appear significant, but the strike leadership persuaded the rebels of their acceptability, and hostilities ceased. Twenty two people had been killed, most by army and police rifle fire, another seventy five had bullet wounds.

†††

There were persistent stories afterwards that, as the two delegations looked down from the balcony of the Carlton Hotel at the confrontation between them, Bain or another of the labour men had threatened to shoot Botha and Smuts if the police and army fired on the crowd. Both Smuts and Bain later denied the story fiercely. Harry Haynes (remember he was Chairperson of the strike committee) has another take on the story in his letters from 1951…

'What really happened – and I have never before mentioned this to a living soul, with an idea of loyalty to the strike committee, of which I was chairman as perhaps you know – is that after we had drafted the conditions of settlement (which I wrote, as being the best penman) and selected our representatives to go to the Carlton, Jimmy Hindman – drunk, as he usually was – produced a small Webley and swore that he would shoot Botha if they refused to sign. At this bravado we all laughed. The pistol, which we found to be unloaded, was taken from him, and the deputation left with our blessings. Not one member was armed.'

What an intriguing thought – the possibility of the assassination of one or both Smuts and Botha! The history of South Africa would have been radically different. Any one of Harry Haynes' strike committee was in a position to carry out such an act, indeed one had seriously contemplated it. What the agreement showed was that the trade unionists, having reached the top table, were happy just to be there. They had reached the apex of their power and were unable and unwilling to push through to more substantial concessions. Was it a lack of courage? Was it a lack of political know-how? Was it simply rebellion for rebellion's sake? Harry Haynes' continued activism would hold the answer to these questions.

†††

A short six months later, in January 1914, the Federation of Trade Unions backed the railway-men who were threatened by the government with layoffs, in a call for another general strike. Smuts, with a little more experience of labour matters under his belt, immediately brought 10,000 troops to the Rand and declared martial law. What was Harry up to now? He was sent to Witbank, to bring out the coalminers there. He took up residence in a hotel, but his activity was short-lived by Smuts' declaration of martial law under which the entire strike leadership countrywide, including Harry, was arrested. As he hadn't committed any crime Harry was simply confined in a hotel room. He described his arrest...

†††

He said, 'I awoke with a start and sat up suddenly. Someone had certainly banged the door or window. I heard a shuffling of feet outside, and then,'

'Fix bayonets!' came the word of command, and my trained ear told me, by the ragged manner in which the order was obeyed, that I was about to become an important captive of the Defence Force. A firm step sounded upon the stoep, then came the anticipated rap upon the door:

'Open, in the King's name,' said a voice.

'Come in, don't be shy,' I invited, and a pause followed. Then, 'Do you intend to resist?' came the voice again, this time in a threatening tone.

'Don't be silly!' I remonstrated, 'I'm in my pyjamas!'

At this the door was flung open, and a young Dutch officer (Lieut. Kruger) in brand new uniform, drawn sword in hand, appeared before my curious gaze.

'Good morning!' I greeted him, 'how are you?'

For some inscrutable reason he seemed to be annoyed with me and did not return my salutation. Instead, he blurted out:

'You're under arrest.'

'What on earth for?'

'Come on, get out of bed and come along. I don't want to use violence,' was the only reply vouchsafed, and two C.I.D. men (decent chaps) sidled past him into the room and stood looking down at me from the bedside.

'Come on, Harry, play the game,' said one of them. 'It's no good riding the goat.'

'Of course I'll play the game,' I replied, 'but give me a chance to get dressed.'

'No, no,' broke in the officer, 'you can dress yourself on the station.'

'Then I won't come unless you carry me,' I said. 'What will the ladies of Witbank say if I walk through the streets in pyjamas?'

The detectives laughed, which appeared further to annoy the young officer, and he gave orders to his squad to come in and take me.

'What about my kit?' I inquired.

'We'll bring that along,' said the detective, who had spoken first, and they did – 'that's how I lost my new slippers!'

†††

Harry had done his second bit of time at Smuts' expense, albeit in the Imperial Hotel in Middelburg. But a far worse situation was the consequence of his radicalism and high-profile. He was persona non grata in the mining industry. In fact he couldn't get a job anywhere, and he now had a wife and two children back at the rented semi-detached in Queen St, Malvern, Johannesburg. The family situation was desperate. His eldest daughter Irene (Jimmy) tells it like this …'I remember once, with great joy I picked up a silver coin which I thought was a shilling. I took it home to my mother who on closer inspection noticed that it was an Indian coin (perhaps already called a rupee) which had the King's head printed on the one side, just like our shillings did. So my mother told me to go down to the store, and buy a loaf of bread with it. Put the coin down on the counter with the King's head upwards, she said. After having got the loaf I was running out of the store when the shopkeeper called after me' –

'You forgot your change'– 'I couldn't get out of there quick enough! Plus I got a sixpence change! Although the battle for my parents to feed us was constant, we were still mostly happy. My brother and I bred rabbits in a hutch out back, and we could never understand why their numbers didn't expand as dramatically as we expected – we only found out later that the missing rabbits were in our bellies!'

Harry did eventually get a job, as a conductor on the trams on the line from town along Jules Street to the end of the road. He stuck at it for a year. Then he was offered a job in Durban through a family contact and the family headed off to a very primitive Durban of 1917. An auspicious date. Lenin had just brought the Bolsheviks to power, creating the first workers' communist state, the Union of Soviet Socialist Republics (USSR). Harry practised his political passions outside of working hours, involving himself in the organized labour community in Durban, which culminated in an extraordinary event…

†††

THE DURBAN SOVIET.

This was the only Soviet ever formed outside of the USSR, and lasted all of three days. The date was 9th January, 1920. The Municipal Employers' Association called its members out on strike. A Council of Action was formed, and who else but Harry Haynes was co-opted onto its leadership. For Harry Durban was different from Jo'burg. He said …'if invited to a musical evening I never knew what to take – a hymn-book or a cork-screw, and similarly, if requested to address a meeting of strikers, I was always in doubt what to speak about – the brotherhood of man or the war of classes. Sometimes I tried both and pleased, and antagonized everybody. On another occasion he quoted the great philosopher Emerson, who said: …'people should not live where bananas grow.' This quote is indeed true, although not in so few words.

The Council of Action put together an audacious plan to seize control of the Town Council of Durban. The plan included capturing the port, deporting the councillors to the Seychelles (as the British had deported Boers to Madagascar after the Boer War), and the immediate surrender of the 'capitalist class'. Rank and file members were sceptical but Harry ...'bullied and cajoled them into listening patiently to a full exposition of the plan until eventually they were persuaded that, with certain modifications, the thing was workable, which after, as is usual in such cases, they waxed fanatically enthusiastic.' The certain modifications were that the Town Councillors would not be deported to the Seychelles (too expensive), and that the surrender of the capitalist class would be postponed until the effect of the proposed coup had been observed.

The Town Hall of Durban was indeed occupied, a piece of red flannel was hoisted over the building to mark the workers' success, the town council was fired, the new bosses started up the council services ... albeit with the same civil service as before but without their evicted political masters. It lasted three days before an accommodation with the old administration was reached and things returned to normal.

The Natal Advertiser, under the headline 'THE SOVIET LEAVES VISITING CARDS' put the matter in a nutshell: ...'The whole purpose of yesterday's coup is, we think, easily explained. It was a preliminary call on the borough; a sort of Soviet visiting card with the understanding that a prolonged visit may be made later.'

Harry's left-wing agitation and political work was still not past its zenith, even though Harry himself was getting long in the tooth for a revolutionary. The effective life of a rebel is often not a prolonged one. Lenin was cut short through a stroke, Trotsky was stopped with an ice axe blow to the skull still as a relatively young man albeit exiled, Che Guevara was warned by the Americans that they were coming for him ...Bobby Sands starved to death ...Steve Biko was bludgeoned to death ...and of course there is the odd exception that proves the rule. But by the time the rebel reaches forty years old, the revolutionary zeal seems to take on a less attractive and entirely desperate meaning and appearance. 'Failure' becomes its name. Your common or garden rebel has long since either capitulated through disillusion or depletion of youthful enthusiasm. And that is assuming of course that along the way no other responsibilities of life have been taken on…

Harry was now thirty-five years old. His family was a wife and six kids strong, including my father born in 1917, all needing assistance with the task of living and growing up. There were now serious demands more pressing than rebellion, but Harry couldn't resist one last hurrah, and very fitting that he should choose the issue of the support of the poor to go out with a bang. He had, from his earliest years looked on humanity, rich and poor, but especially the poor, as fellow men and worthy of respect, 'I'll make you say 'sir' to a ragman,' was one of his father's sayings Harry never forgot.

Due to the pressures of his activist commitments in Durban, Harry was unable to make the Rand revolt in 1922, but by 1923 he was back in Jo'burg and plotting what turned out to be his final significant act of rebellion. It became known as…

†††

THE CHAIN GANG.

Harry put a cunning plan together for a demonstration in Cape Town's parliament where once again General Jan Smuts (now Prime Minister) would be doing his work. On behalf of the Unemployment Committee of South Africa he planned with two others to enter parliament, chain themselves to railings, and harangue all in parliament about the plight of the unemployed and destitute in South Africa.

First off, he had to borrow the money for the train fare, as he was unemployed again. A friend lent him some chain and he headed for Cape Town. The three gained access to Parliament with the help of a sympathetic labour MP, and entered the House in overcoats underneath which were the chains and locks. Colonel Denys Reitz was at the box in full cry when Harry rose, having chained himself to the railing, and began his thundering oratory in support of the poor…

Newspaper reports of the time wrote of the effect of this demo in Parliament: …'Had a bombshell been thrown the consternation could not have been greater. (Prime Minister) Smuts was livid with rage, and when Haynes, sarcastically referring to him as 'the world's greatest statesman.' Smuts got up, threw his papers down, and stalked out of the House. With four policemen and two attendants at him, Haynes continued his harangue until throttled off'…

The police arrived in force – every available policeman had been rushed to the House, and attempts were made to release the self-made prisoners while the basements, drains and precincts were searched for dynamite. At last a mechanic was obtained from a local garage who succeeded in cutting through the padlocks with a hacksaw. That ended the episode.

The 'chain gang' received an enthusiastic welcome at various meetings they addressed. The Grand Theatre was totally inadequate to accommodate the attendance, and thousands failed to get in. Harry Haynes bluntly told the assembled workers that Smuts' only achievement worth recording was that of capturing a Fordsburg lavatory with 60,000 troops (the Rand Revolt), and called upon everyone present to stand and give three rousing cheers for the World Revolution. The response was deafening. The following day, the send-off from Cape Town station was something to be remembered. The Communist Choir led the singing of The Red Flag and the Internationale. Speeches were made, and Harry Haynes was carried shoulder high to the train to the strains of 'For he's a jolly good fellow'.

So there we have it. An ancestor hung for treason, a great-great grandparent releasing Fenian leaders and shooting policemen in the process and a grandfather fermenting revolution in the early South Africa. I couldn't help but feel a sense of admiration for Harry, of a life lived to its full through extraordinary times. Was it not Marx who said there was no point in understanding social movement of our time, but to act on it. Harry certainly did that, he fought for the poor, he managed to ignore the fact that he was one. But his family was never able to forget their hardship. Harry was on his own mission, the rightness of which he was intellectually convinced of, from which he was not to be persuaded, and for which he argued to his dying day.

Did I like the Harry Haynes I had come to know through the learning of his story? He was arrogant, he was pig-headed and his necessary dogmatism often hurt those closest to him. He also had a sense of humour which would have made him more sympathetic if it had been more self-deprecating. Many of the Haynes clan have similar temperament, including myself, which is sometimes a terror to admit. It would only be fair to conclude with Harry on one of his favourite quotations, one which says it all:

†††

> ***Life is a jest, and all things show it;.***
> ***I thought so once, and now I know it.***
> *Epitaph of John Gay (1685–1732).*

Be all this as it may, Timothy Russell Haynes, grandson of Harry Walter and all the rest, had no choice but to proceed to do what he was always going to do.

The Haynes family group 1900, Harry just returned in his Boer War uniform.

Harry Haynes adressing Socialist meeting in Albert Park Durban 1920.

1913 strike leadership with Mary Fitzgerald.

A CRUCIAL MOMENT.

Pender Tole

Left to right Standing: Messrs. ~~Watson~~, Waterston, ~~Nicol~~ and Clark (Town Councillor). Seated: Messrs. Mason, Haynes, Bain and Dingwall (T.C.). Photo by Linton.

The strike committee Kleinfontein 1913

H. W. Haynes, chairman of the Benoni Strike committee.

Police charging the crowd on Johannesburg Market Square.

Police charging the crowd on Johannesburg Market Square.

he Men in Chai

Vill The Government Not List

V. C. WOUDBERG,
Ex-Civil Servant,
Union of S. Africa.

HARRY HAYNES.

H. J. McCARTHY,
Ex-Officer of the
S.A.S.C.

ie three men in chains who demonstrated in the House of Assembly a
t's sitting, 18th June, 1923, on behalf of the thousands of unempl

'The Chain Gang' protest over poverty in Parliament Cape Town 1923.

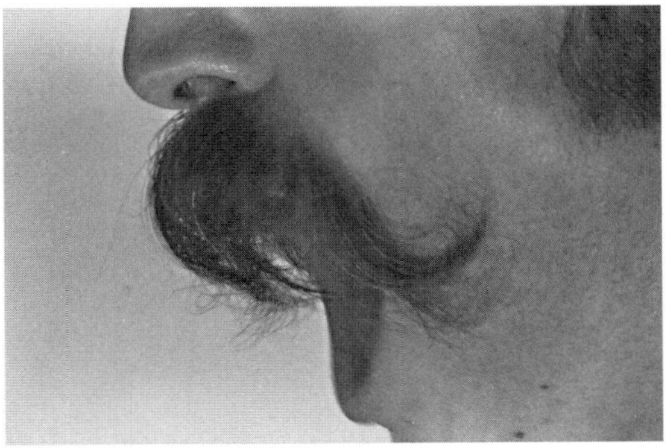

STORY 4

AARON, THE MANGLED LEG AND A NEW KARMA.

I met a man named Aaron with a mangled leg. In my little shared house in Harfield Village, each Sunday friends would pop in to share a big pot of vegetarian stew, meat being outside my meagre first job budget. The friends joined me in spooning directly out of the pot, all huddled together on the double mattress that was the bed on the floor. A flagon or two of 'Tas', very cheap Cape wine, washed the bean ensemble down. Call it my first stab at the grown up Sunday lunch. We were now free to choose our own ways of doing things. Hence the bean thing and mattress on the floor – infinitely preferable to a proper bed and good food at a table with knives and forks under parental umbrellas back at the family ranch. And the informality allowed for friends of friends: Aaron was one of these.

He had massive scars down the length of his leg, large enough to have totally disfigured its shape and rendered its function hugely imperfect. He limped heavily, I remember he even used a stick. As the leg was bared for all to see, this being summer , it immediately became the subject of discourse amongst the luncheoners. The discourse suited Aaron perfectly, another personality might well have tried to disguise the disfigurement and make out that they were as whole and as perfectly formed as the next person. Not Aaron, and for good reason. He was on a quest.

Aaron was no Camel man, in shape or in temperament. In fact he was the opposite. Short, dark, clever, introspective. But there was no law that said you had to be a Camel man to go to the Okavango Delta, Botswana, where wild animals walked free, roaming the plains looking for lunch.

Aaron had been holidaying with some friends on the edge of the Okavango swamps. He and his party bedded down for the night, in sleeping bags around the camp fire, with no other protection against the carnivores looking for meat to sustain their lives. Just at the edge of the circle of light created by the fire, was a circle of yellow eyes, bodiless eyes, moving, winking, receding and re–appearing. They could hear the coughing of lion, the rasping, guttural wheeze of lion on the move, with the occasional roar of regal assertion. It was a terrifying experience. A braai fire, suited to the cooking of chops, all of a sudden seemed hopelessly inadequate against the power and brutality of the lion and hyena out for an entire body if they could get it. But the visitors into this animal kingdom were there to experience this very thing. And there was no way of escaping now. They had to get through the night. Keeping the fire going was all the defence they had. But, inconceivably, they fell asleep.

Aaron woke to an excruciating pain in his leg. Instantly gathering his senses he realized he was being dragged through the bush by a lion attached to his leg through the sleeping bag. It was an awakening into hell. A sound exploded in his gut and found escape in a blood curling bellow. His body lashed out, his fists pummelled the huge head fixed to his leg, he grabbed at passing bush stumps, ripping his hands, and he tried to roll over in escape. The lion was silent, but the rustle and scratch of his bag and body through the bush gushed through his ears. The teeth ripping the flesh of his leg held his life in a vice. His own voice was the sound of a tree falling in a forest with no-one to hear it… after some distance, miraculously, the lion released his leg and fled into the deeper bush. Aaron's friends had woken to the disappearing human screams, and in disarray grabbed instruments of protection, a stick, a knife, and charged off in the direction of the sound in complete fear and panic. They brought him back to the camp and applied a tourniquet of rope to his leg. Incredibly he survived the ordeal, and still kept his leg, albeit mangled.

That was the story that Aaron told us sitting aboard my mattress. Of course there were many questions from the horrified eating party, some of whom could not eat even their meatless meal with that leg, now with its awful explanation, stretched out on the mattress before them. The scars were still blue purple, the colour of newness. The image of the freshly described macabre scene in the minds of all was too ghastly to be easily dislodged. But Aaron had moved onto a different aspect of the whole event. He was asking of himself and the assembled folk why this grisly occurrence had happened to him. Someone of practical and unsympathetic bent, said that 'if you had been part of an 80,000 crowd at a football match and were hit on the head by a bottle, you might well ask why me? But if you go into the jungle, a thing made of meat, and you sit with a bunch of different varieties of carnivore and you get eaten, the answer to 'why me' is fairly obvious.' Aaron was totally unconvinced. He wanted to know why it had happened to HIM, as opposed to one his fellow tourists. In other words there was substantially more of an explanation than that he was in the right place at the wrong time. There must be a higher, a deeper explanation and he had embarked on a quest to find it.

He had started out with the Rabbi, although his Judaism had lapsed following his barmitzvah, but the rabbi's advice that G-d did have a reason and purpose in putting him through this ordeal, but we mere mortals could not explain what that might be, did not satisfy him. Aaron checked out Christianity. 'Jews for Jesus' had recently appeared and was all the rage at that time. Had he repented of his sins? they wanted to know. He went into Buddhism – too passive although he liked the 'karma' thing. He stopped by Jehovah's Witnesses, for whom the world was to end in 2000, so this question was too insignificant for them, given that the whole planet would soon be going down. The shrink was more concerned about how Aaron himself felt about it, so no answers there. He changed the shrink. Same thing. He had gone to psychologists of different persuasions: the Freudian, the Jungian, the old style. He even met one who advised he try some Electro Shock Therapy to dislodge his 'why me' obsession. He tried Transcendental Meditation, thinking he could at least still have the thing in his mind but not think about it. He couldn't.

At the time of our lunch Aaron was trying African voodoo. He was on his second witchdoctor, a white man nogal, who was throwing bones and presenting various potions to drink which were not very tasty. The ancestors were obviously upset. By what? With whom? The good doctor, albeit witch, could not get a handle on Aaron's ancestors so different to those with which he was familiar. So the project went nowhere.

He delved into Jainism, Taoism, Scientology, Hinduism, Gnosticism, Ordo Templi Orientis, Ecclesia Gnostica Catholica, Freemasonry, Hinduism, Spinoza, Korjybski's non-Aristolian logic, and finally Rudolf Steiner's anthroposophy. So much did Aaron like the sound of anthroposophy that he went to the Rudolf Steiner college in Sussex, England, principally (I imagine) to study this aspect of their teaching… 'The individual's karmic condition eventually leads to a choice of parents, physical body, disposition and capacities… and includes karmically chosen tasks for the future life'.

I lost touch with Aaron, until a few years later he contacted me, and I invited him over to another meal at a house in Balham, London, once again a house in which I'd hired a room. This time I did have a table and chairs, and once again I invited a few friends over, one of whom was a Nigerian nursing sister who lived next door. We had in common our Africanness – her complaints about the racism she was experiencing in London from the white British, me regaling her with the horrors of Apartheid in South Africa.

The happy party was seated for the dinner at the dinner party and within seconds we were onto the subject of racism and Apartheid and Aaron was espousing his views on the plight of the non-white South African. 'Of course nothing can or should be done about Apartheid,' he was saying.

'Why so? Why not?' asked the incredulous Nigerian woman. Everybody pricked up their ears.

'Well because the lives and situation of the oppressed people were chosen by themselves, it is in their karma, as it was in mine to have my leg ruined by the lion.'

All hell broke loose at the dinner party, and minutes later the Nigerian woman, screaming principally at me, had left the premises. I was angry enough to eject Aaron as well. Neither of them did I ever see again.

I'd had my fill of karma, meditators, enlightened consciousness, gods, supernaturals in any form, people who at the end of the day were as disreputable and power hungry, as ambitious, as materialistic, as violent, as dishonest as any politician. I was as disillusioned with the disciples, the footsoldiers as much as the personalities who were the guiding lights of the consciousness movements. My genealogy suggested that rebellion was in my genes, so it looked like politics was to be the route I would go. And ironic then that I should become a footsoldier myself.

Parallel with the heyday of the consciousness movement's arose the new politics of the left. The resurrection of Marx and Engels, of Lenin and Trotsky without Stalin, updated by the new intellectuals. In the late seventies and early eighties in England alone there emerged eighty or so 'loony left' political movements. And of course for the truly enraged people out there, there were the Angry Brigade, the Red Brigade, Baader

'Memory's truth… has its own special kind. It selects, eliminates, alters, exaggerates, minimizes, glorifies, and vilifies also; but in the end it creates its own reality, its heterogeneous but usually coherent version of events; and no sane human being ever trusts someone else's version more than his own.' Salman Rushdie.

Meinhof, the IRA, the PLO, the Sandinistas, Che Guevara/Fidel Castro, the Mau Mau, in fact almost every country on every continent had a liberation movement, and usually with an office in London.

Balham didn't last long and I repaired to a squat near the Oval. A window was open in a perfectly preserved and empty flat. We climbed through it, changed the lock on the front door and it was home sweet home. And finally, the politics.

The spotlight is on what to think... ?

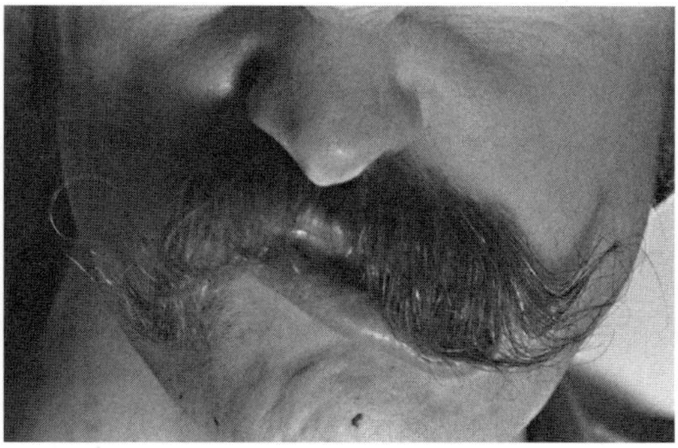

STORY 5

THE BRITISH REVOLUTIONARY LEFT.

How… do I find meaning and purpose in life? How does a mere and gross materialist, with no expectation of a life to come, decide what, if anything, is worth caring about? *(Christopher Hitchens)*

In comparison with life for a twenty-something kid in South Africa, everything in London was stimulating and different. This was the late 1970s, with a gray Britain of dilapidated council housing estates, moribund politics and trade unions which had been toiling unreformed since the Second World War. I had jetted in to London just before the season of strikes and other demonstrations of discontent. So it was ironic that I found Britain new, fresh and exciting. It served as a horrible indictment of what living in South Africa was like at the time, even for a white privileged kid like myself.

In England there was so much to do and explore, and then there was the rest of Europe just over the channel. I had to do menial work to keep myself in food and shelter, so the idea of South Africa, the 'struggle' and revolutionary politics had receded onto the back-burner of my existence.

It came to the fore again through a chance meeting at Finsbury Park tube station. Returning from work one afternoon I bumped into another 'exile', a friend from university with whom I had lost contact, after his graduation and my dropout. He had then disappeared from South Africa, a short while before a large Sunday Times article appeared, complete with Che Guavara look-a-like picture of himself, in 1975. A new revolutionary organization had surfaced in Europe called 'Okhela'. This new outfit was committed to the overthrow not only of the evil regime of Apartheid, but also the entire capitalist system. As with many new formations, 'Okhela' was sunk in Cape Town, shortly after its founder Breyten Breytenbach sailed in on a recruitment drive amongst white lefties. Breyten had been arrested and in time went to gaol, but here was one of HIS recruits at Finsbury Park tube station, about to recruit ME.

What I didn't know then, but learnt after 1985 when Breytenbach wrote his book on the subject, was that my friend at Finsbury Park station had, in Breytenbach's opinion not exactly supported his cause in his trial. Breytenbach wrote that he 'went out of (his) way to wag (his) tail and ingratiate (himself) with the prosecution to the extent that (he) would invent and ascribe intentions to me which did not even exist, with allusions to spying, to violent terroristic activities... I learned (that he) was suffering from uncontrolled bowel movements, and appeared in an ill-smelling, rumpled suit. On his way back from the witness box, passing by the Dock where I sat, I couldn't refrain from advising him to have his suit cleaned.' Breytenbach spent eight years in gaol, some of it in hearing distance to the gallows in Pretoria Central prison, and my friend may well have contributed to putting him there.

†††

After a sceptical greeting between myself and my man at Finsbury Park tube station, he asked me what I was doing in London. His question was politically loaded.

'Nothing,' I said, a little embarrassed. After the level of commitment we had once known of each other as student activists, it would have been expected that I would be 'doing something'. And then by way of excuse I added: 'Been to a couple of ANC (African National Congress) meetings.'

'Are you working with those petit bourgeois idiots?' he asked. The wording of the question spoke volumes of his present political affiliations.

I had been to one openly advertised ANC meeting. It was addressed by Oliver Tambo and attended by a small motley crew of ANC exiles. It was totally boring and uninspiring. I was on my own; a twenty-something long-haired unconfident white male complete with South African accent. A big Indian or African woman seated in the row in front of me kept on turning round and looking me over. Then she started asking me intimidating questions like what I was doing there and where did I come from, and when we had to rise and sing Nkosi Sikelel', my performance under her beady eye was woefully inadequate. It was clear that she thought I was a South African security agent, and she was priming herself to perform a public exposure. My body went cold at the thought of how I would cope with such a scene. I would probably stammer and stutter the truth: that I was in fact, just another inhibited soul who felt there was dreadful injustice in South Africa and was looking to express my opposition to it. Which was why I was at the meeting. A pathetic explanation when I could be a white cop on some well-paid undercover work. I took the coward's route and knocked over a couple of chairs in my haste to get to the exit and escape into the dark London streets.

'No,' I said to my old acquaintance, thinking not of 'petit bourgeois idiots' but of that ANC meeting. 'Wouldn't touch them with a barge-pole.'

'Why don't you come and talk to us then?' he asked.

'Who's us?' I asked. 'What do you do?'

'Ag, just a few people thinking about an organization,' he said vaguely. We made a plan some days later to meet over a pint in the pub, the first of many meetings in which he and occasionally one of his chums, would talk to me of politics and our reasons for living.

†††

From this motley crew, I cottoned onto the idea that if you had South African origins, to get access to this particular 'organization' with the beginner's title of 'candidate member', it was a good thing to dislike the African National Congress. I learnt that The Freedom Charter was not a revolutionary but rather a social democratic document, therefore the ANC were not anti-capitalist. My new organization distinguished itself from the rest of the British loony left by being vociferously anti-ANC. This position was enough to locate the fledgling organization on the radical left of the loony left. That's seriously left. The point was that on every issue, one had to have a pure position, more pure than the next lot. So while I thought the ANC was maybe a little soft, a lot of my previous associates who had voluntarily exiled themselves to the UK were in this 'organization'. It felt like, well, if they hated the ANC, there had to be a reason. My newly turned up old comrades were all graduates of prestigious educational institutions all over the world with many and varied degrees and post degrees. I was a dropout, so I had to give their analysis the benefit of the doubt. By the way, for political correctness the 'organization' was not actually even an 'organization'. It was a 'tendency' to an organization, until certain ducks were in a row. Which ducks those were I never found out, but Lenin and Trotsky were substantially involved in the definition, as were certain numbers of bodies to form a re-educated quorum big enough to constitute a party rather than a tendency to a party. Polemics had arrived in my life.

After some weeks, I was summoned to an interview at a secret location, a squat down the Camberwell road. To interview me were a couple of my previous pals and another South African whom I didn't know. I presumed he was there to give an independent assessment, free from any subjective bias that might arise from a reunion of past comrades who might be tempted to recount and sentimentalize past times together. I was to learn that emotion was a nyet in this new, more serious revolutionary movement.

Things seemed to go well. Knowing what I had to do, I used the words social democratic and revolutionary and ANC in the right configuration. They said I had a lot to learn but at least I had come to the right address. I was then ordered to a meeting with a rep from top management, sorry er… Politburo.

The meeting took place in a Wimpy restaurant in Brixton. I was surprised. I thought that in London the 'greasy spoon' café on every High Street and under every railway arch would be the preferred eating destination of the working class. But this was working class management class so it was the garish red of Wimpy that greeted myself and my final assessor. She was thin, tall, blonde short hair, ordinary specs (not the round Trotsky type all the rage at that time) and elegantly dressed. No jeans and bovver boots for this revolutionary. She was a classy dame. She put me straight in my place. She told me that I was a petit bourgeois idiot who needed sustained and substantial education. Worse, I was a man. While these were huge impediments, they would not necessarily stand in the way; some middle class idiot men like me had already been turned into useful comrades. It was all down to my effort and commitment.

I noticed the red plastic tomato sauce receptacle, with dirty dribble down the side, uncleaned for some days. The grubby tan mustard dispenser with half the descriptive piece printed on its side worn off. My eyes drifted to her vibrating tongue, the colour a cross between the red of the tomato sauce and the yellow mustard. My mind was wandering. I pulled back with effort to being a revolutionary. She told me about the chauvinism of the British working class. I learnt that the real enemy of my new Communist 'tendency' was the Labour Party because it was the Labour Party that organized and funneled the chauvinism of the British working class into support of capitalism. This had to be broken by breaking the working class from the Labour Party. I started slurping the last of my peach melba. She slowed and looked at me disapprovingly. I shut up the slurping. She resumed in her deep, officious, well-bred businesslike voice and manner of speaking. The tendency would use two issues to confront and break the British working class from their racism and support of the British imperialist state. The two issues were racism at home, the white British working class must support non-British people especially those whom the ruling class had brought in from the diaspora to do the dirty jobs capitalism required. And secondly, to break the British working class from supporting the British state's continued and vicious subjugation of Northern Ireland.

She stopped, her pinky finger standing erect in the air as she sipped elegantly the last of her black coffee.

'Oh yes,' I said.

I thought I could do worse than be told what to do and how to do it by someone like her, and I might even learn something different along the way. In my life to date I'd not been a confident extrovert and maybe it was because I was a petit bourgeois idiot. It rolled off the tongue quite easily when you got used to it, and it might turn out to be my exact problem. It sure was a term that was used a lot around the 'tendency'.

'And by the way,' she said, 'from now your name will be… er… Simon… ah… Peters.' So I was christened there and then, with only Wimpy as witness. 'Simon Peters'. My new name sounded biblical rather than revolutionary but then I was thankful it wasn't to be Leon, Che or Fidel. For the rest, well, she was just fascinating.

And then came her parting shot… 'And get that hair properly cut, we're not a bunch of hippies here.' Oh God, she was gorgeous. Forgetting where I was, what I was and what I was supposed to be, I said with a little too much enthusiasm, too much excitement in my voice: 'Yes, ma'am.' It just came out. It's what we used to call the teachers at school but now it sounded like some horrible B-grade movie line.

She looked at me like I was a smelly piece of shit she could not dislodge from the grooves in her shoe, which of course, I was.

'We're comrades from now on,' she said icily, clearly getting a little exasperated.

'Yes, sir… eh… sorry… comrade,' I said to her back as she huffily left the Wimpy, leaving me to pick up the tab.

So that was how it began. I was in…

I was told to buy some copies of Lenin Marx Trotsky Engels, all available in cheap printed editions at alternative bookstores on every High Street and to be read under instruction from my minder, a full member of the tendency, and in anticipation of a workshop to be held for the full tendency in session at the University of London. And of course my life of demonstrations, pickets, sales and odd jobs at the office in Brixton was in loco.

The program of the tendency sounded like a tough project. One that
would immediately invite most British people, let alone the working class, to smash you over the head before you'd opened your foreign mouth, even if you were white. When Lord Mountbatten's 'head and shoulders' (a sick joke about an anti-dandruff soap at the time) were found on a county Sligo beach, we were out there telling Brits that it wasn't a bad thing. When Robert Mugabe was winning the war against the British white colonialists, we were trying to get the working class to celebrate with us.

But hey, I was always up for a challenge.

†††

Of course, as is the nature of all organizations big and small, the head honcho was banging all the women. This was, I concluded, the real reason why there were so many loony left organizations in Britain at that time. Rather than military overthrows or executions, when one felt a right to head honcho status, one simply resigned and set up shop next door, taking as many of the women as one could recruit. Even with the rise of the movement for the liberation of women, the traditional practice and rights of the head honcho were still not being threatened. Ironically, the only woman leader of a political party was Margaret Thatcher in the Conservative Party. The result of this practice was that in its heyday, the late '70s and early '80s, there existed in excess of seventy organizations in England alone that fell into the 'loony left' category.

This is exactly how our 'tendency' was born, and the political pretext for separation in Britain in 1979 happened to be the ANC. Every one of the other seventy organizations joined the anti-Apartheid struggle through supporting the ANC. Not ours. Having identified the Freedom Charter as a social democratic not revolutionary document, it opposed the ANC and set up another organization. But more importantly, our head honcho had recruited a number of female comrades into the upper echelons of his new organization. He would make sure that all the new recruits were personally instructed by himself as well.

Although I was a brand-new candidate member, it only took five minutes to find some other comrades who had some complaint or other with the political positions of the organization and the personnel who managed them. We would meet in the pub and have a little laugh about it all. And as so often in my life, I became part of this little counter-revolutionary revolutionary cell on the sidelines.

One of the members of this group was a home girl from South Africa. She told us that she'd had her turn in the head honcho's bed. He treated her and the occasion as yet another workshop in which he was imparting some pure and proper positions in yet another type of revolutionary activity. So he spoke the whole way through. His accent was a cross between American and European.

'So now I am going to put this in here, and you vill notice that you feel something over there. Now if I put my finger in there as well, then you vill be feeling something else. Walla. Ve have to inwestigate all possibilities. So roll over and ve do it the other way around.' Apparently this was all part of the dialectic, all part of the art of investigation by discussion and practice. Discussion alone is an abstraction. All discussion must have a material consequence. It has to be grounded in the doing. Hence dialectical materialism. Hence the finger in the bum. After petit bourgeois, and democratic centralism, dialectical materialism was the next term of great importance. We were learning a whole new language in the process. And why not? We were after all building a whole New World.

Of course the head honcho could afford to impart this largesse as often as possible. After all he was a head honcho who took a personal interest in the development of the learners in his corporation. Who wouldn't? Only an idiot hell-bent on destroying his own organization. I witnessed, over a week, just how much of this type of building work he actually got through. As a carpenter, the only one in the organization (the rest were intellectuals) I was called upon to refit his whole council flat with cupboards and bookshelves.

The head honcho had shipped his old mum over from Eastern Europe and ensconced her in a pretty dingy council flat in Lambeth. She seemed happy enough. Her role and function was to procure and cook food, clean the flat and the clothes of the boy king. She was a master at these tasks. She performed her job to perfection and got only bad mouth and manners in return for her efforts from her anti-sexist pro-workerist son, indeed it appeared the only person she had in the world. The food she served me up in the middle of a carpentry working day was magnificent. All original goulashes and sausage.

It was a three bedroom flat, one room sumptuously furnished in deep red, thick velvet curtaining, with the bed as centre-point to the room, which was so big that little else could fit into the small space. My job was to build some cupboards just above head height. I worked in the bedroom in the mornings. The leading body was home for lunch, having endured a tough morning in the revolutionary office or lecturing at university (his day job, which he kept). With him would be a comrade to whom he would be administering some personal tuition in the afternoon. I would then be dispatched to the next room to work on the bookshelves there, and occasionally heard a little moan through the wall as a particular piece of wisdom on the terrors of imperialism was well taken. That was of course only when the comrade was not English. Somehow the English comrades zipped up their lips when learning the finer points of how developed countries fucked undeveloped ones, how the capitalist pig fucked the worker.

When the revolutionary medicine had been given and taken and it was all over, Mum would be summoned to provide some refreshment. Then the comrades would be gone and as was my particular habit, I would find some pretext to enter the room and scout around for some morsel that the leading body might have left - a scrap of paper on which might be written some modern revolutionary verse or a new insight into 'Kronstadt, why did it happen?' – but all that I ever found was some tome lying closed on the bedside table and the bed all messed up. I wondered why it was necessary to do this study surreptitiously under the bedclothes by candlelight, but then I remembered my own new name and how above all else, security considerations were paramount. The bourgeoisie had spies everywhere.

Of course none of us in the rebellion faction made any progress in the organization. And there were some 'heavy hitters' amongst us, people who'd written books, political tomes, who could give the incumbents a run for their money. Which is why they were with us, sidelined, half ex-communicated, slowly being eased out even though we were only three people and a dog. If it was the Soviet Union we would have been killed. Instead, we just became those that did the legwork, sold the propaganda on the streets before work, after work, at meetings, picket lines, at markets on a Sunday, on council estates. And sometimes we put our physical safety on the line. First in small ways like selling the paper, the propaganda tool of the organization at East Ham tube station, East Ham being a breeding ground for the right wing National Front skinheads and then the more radical British Movement thugs. They didn't appreciate some Reds appearing from under the bed and trying to wear the pyjamas. We were gonna show them that we were harder than the rest of the soft gutless left: the pinkos, the Stalinists, all of them. We were the Trots, the real Trots, the real thing that revolution was all about. But it was just a little annoying putting one's body on the line knowing that the only risk the head honcho was taking with his body was a risk of some over indulgent disease.

Then it got worse. The central committee decided that what was necessary for the advance of dialectical materialism was to get a whole lot more provocative. A series of anti-racism meetings were planned all over east London. The first was to be held in a community hall attached to an old aged home in Canning Town. It was advertised on posters throughout the area and in the local press so that any literate, self respecting racist would have to take exception to it.

The night of the meeting came, as did a build-up of horrifying numbers of fat skinheads with union jack T-shirts, tight denims with braces, Doc Marten boots and tattoos on thick red necks. The management of the old aged home realised they'd been conned into allowing this meeting on their premises, and quite rightly, feeling their inmates were being put at risk, told us to leave.

We phoned head office in Brixton to send re-enforcements fast or we would soon be pulverized and especially to send the leading body who was reputed to be endowed with triple dans, bestowed upon him by the King of Japan. We held out in the foyer of the hall with mad dogs baying for our blood from the outside and a growing gaggle of frantic grannies and gramps trying to eject us from the inside. If only the leading body would arrive and take control of this situation with his dans and his superior politics. He would know what to do and do it. We then looked at our own resources in terms of personnel. Our group consisted largely of the pub renegades and a few other nerds. While to have accused top management of having deliberately stitched us up would be an exaggeration, (this was hardly the charge of the Light Brigade), we did slowly realise that reinforcements would not be forthcoming.

The management of the old age centre had been continuously on the phone to the police, who kept stalling with lack of resources excuses. Clearly they too were quite happy to see these irritating Reds get a bit of a bashing.

We all swallowed deep, formed into a tight squad of twenty with men on the outside and women on the inside (which was probably contrary to regulations) and made a fast break for the nearest tube approximately a mile away. It was one of the worst twenty minutes of my life. The fascists were like hungry wild dogs trying to bring down the body of an antelope. They were darting in throwing punches or kicking at the flanks of the group. The group would take a hit, repulse the attack and keep tight and moving as fast as possible. Fortunately, the skinheads couldn't organise themselves into a sustained attack or we would all have been hospitalised or worse. Eventually we made the tube station nursing only thick lips, bulging noses, sore heads and a few other injured bits.

Top management adjudged our engagement with the opposition at the old age home to be a good start to the organization's anti-racism campaign in the East End of London. This meeting fiasco would be followed up by a more in your face ongoing action against the fascists.

On various estates and in the suburbs of east London where Indians, Pakistanis or Bangladeshis were trying to escape the ghettos around Brick Lane, they were harassed and intimidated, especially by the local fascisti belonging to the National Front or British Movement. This harassment would take the form of broken windows, graffiti, and physical intimidation and assault on the streets. And the odd death. Most of the non-white, non-indigenous population suffered in this way, and because they were isolated and weak they merely had to grin and bear it or move back into the ghettos where their numbers were stronger.

A few meetings were held in Hackney and Mile End to tell the harassed non-whites that we were there to protect them. A number of willing potential participants in our new scheme came forward and one family was chosen as a pilot. Abdul Latif, his wife and small kids lived in a terraced row in Canning Town and were being harassed: rocks through windows, excrement through the letter box and physical assault on the street. They were unable to use the front rooms in the house at all, especially after a rock flying through the window just missed the youngest child sleeping in a cot. The plan was a simple one. We would provide protective personnel for his house and family. We would attack the attackers. While I agreed with the basic philosophic principle that simple is best, I thought that maybe the head honcho and his rocket scientists' might have come up with something slightly more imaginative, given that the numbers game was clearly against us. When I voiced a milder version of this sentiment, I was told I was ignoring the political dimension. It was complicated but I was able to summarise it for myself as 'today political victory in Canning Town (and probably a bashing), tomorrow world power', and this kept me going for another week.

We started spending the evening, then sleeping overnight. With this timetable a confrontation was likely to happen sooner rather than later. It was 9 pm and a lone skinhead was seen sitting on a low fence at the end of the block in the shadow of a bush. Ten minutes later there were two, then four, then five or six. They started horsing about in the road, raucously pushing each other about, shouting and whistling, playing football with a cardboard box. And all the while moving down the road, closer and closer to the Asian house in which we were all camped.

I looked around at our troops. Vaughan P was 29 years old. He had on his duffel coat. He always had on his duffel coat. Remember those camel coloured duffel coats with the 'buttons' that were miniature horn shapes fitted through big loops. Oh, and of course the hood. Which Vaughan P often actually put over his head, 30 years before hoodies became fashionable. I think he thought he looked quite cute in it. He had a miniature head and a small-featured face which was beautifully surrounded by red hair immaculately permed into the pageboy Prince Valiant style which had been all the rage more than two decades earlier. His life until very recently had been funded by the dole, his accommodation by the local council. He had finally secured a job in the Homerton hospital. It was to collect together the belongings of those that had unfortunately succumbed, pack them neatly in a plastic bag, record the contents and store them in anticipation of collection by next of kin. It was the perfect job for Comrade Vaughan P, and it gave him a new lease of life. He was from thence forward even more pedantic than ever; having once got his small Chihuahua-like teeth into an obscure adjunct to the definition of imperialism, he could not be shaken free. The way in which top management dealt with him was to make him a part of the anti-racist attack squad.

Then there was Andy M. Andy M had thick black-rimmed glasses the weight of which kept pulling them down his nose. His right index finger was fully employed pushing them back. He'd been around the loony left forever, but this organization would be his final resting-place, such was his commitment. A woman comrade, part of our anti-revolutionary, revolutionary cell once told us that she was assigned to a propaganda sales trip at a tube station. As was normal practice. After which, they had gone to the pub. That night she was feeling quite morose as one often did after those sales trips. After all, suffering abuse from every passer-by at a busy station day in day out, week in week out could finally take its toll on even the most optimistic of personalities. She buried her depression in a few too many drinks. As she was quite wobbly on her feet Comrade Andy M kindly walked her home. At three in the morning she awoke with the very common post drunken condition called dry mouth. She was shocked to discover that around the loin area of the bed it was all wet. Surely she could not have been that out of control as to urinate in the bed? She crawled to the bathroom where she drank a gallon of water. She returned rather wobbly to the room to find the bedside light on and Andy M propped up on the pillows. 'Mary,' he said, 'do wage increases cause inflation?' … 'Fuck off out my flat this instant, you pathetic git,' she shouted in a hysterical fury, aggravating her already pained head, and throwing her future advancement up the ranks of the organization to the wind.

Sabine N was there. German royal blood flowed in her veins. She was older than the rest of us, with a host of qualifications behind her name. She was regarded, most especially by herself, as the mother of the organization. She looked upon the rest of us with total patronage on account of the differences in our breeding and education. She was tall, held herself erect and had the highest cheekbones you ever did see. Big wide-apart piercing blue eyes and straight short hair that always looked done even though it was seldom touched. This all had the effect of her being absolutely beautiful in a regal sort of way, provided she was not underweight and overstressed. If she was underweight and overstressed, her eyes took on a blackened hue and sunk as completely as the Bismark, creating the visage of a ghoul from Transylvania. So what the hell was she doing in this house of the Bangladeshis?

Well it happened like this… Sabine, back at head office, was the head honcho's official girlfriend (although I merely put this in understandable parlance, girlfriend was very definitely not the right adjective for Sabine, firstly because she was revolutionary, and secondly because she was Sabine). We were all just simple comrades. As already mentioned, at that particular time the head honcho had a lot of other diversions, should we call them, on his plate, should we call it. And whenever that was the case, he shipped Sabine out of the way. On this occasion the business of the organization demanded that she keep an eye on the attack squad in east London.

With the fascists now barely more than the thickness of the Latif front door away, the only aspect of the revolutionary forces that could be guaranteed was that they would be committed to the end.

Not so Fred the spy. He was another 'exiled' South African white comrade whose past was a shady shade of white, and whose present activities outside the organization were highly suspect. For this he was nicknamed 'Fred the spy'. This kind of unfortunate reputation feeds upon itself. Where did it come from? And having acquired it, how does one shake it off? So while his fighting abilities might have rated higher than the others, if there was anything to his reputation he might just stab you in the back when none of the other comrades were looking.

Thank God, the besieged Latif family were not going to rely on this pathetic vanguard force of the British Red Army. They had shipped in a number of cousins, nephews, uncles, everyone in fact introduced as a distant relation, and some of them, judging by the facial scars on exhibition had had experience of this sort of thing.

As the group of skinheads moved closer and closer down the road, the distant relatives repaired to the kitchen to lay hands on whatever implement might offer some comfort in the coming battle. So the cutlery drawer was the first port of call, and a glistening array of blades was soon spread across the kitchen table. The carving knives proved to be a very popular item, the meat cleavers, although a little bulky were a second choice followed by the smaller blades. We are talking of implements whose very efficiency had already caused controversy in the same terraced rows of London. They were used in the creation of halal meat by the slicing open of the necks of live sheep and goats, the blood of which drained down those white British gutters and caused such a furore among the locals.

Now the relatives were taking no chances, and stood thumbing the edge of their allotted blades, whether purely for theatrical effect or not was difficult to say. These actions had their effect. The revolutionaries were horrified. Sabine, the most senior political rep present, stepped in. 'Hey guys… er… comrades, we're out to stop this intimidation and score a few political points here, not commit bloody murder,' was the gist of what she said. 'No,' said the Bangladeshis, 'we'd like to kill those fat bastards and drain their blood into the gutter before they succeed in killing us.' Sabine had her work cut out persuading them to lay down their arms, using some pretty un-revolutionary argument, I thought. But what did I know. A candidate member in a tendency. In the end it was decided that we had sufficient strength in numbers to go out and give the fascists a hiding without the weapons.

On the given signal, the mob of skinheads on the street that evening must have been startled to see the front door of the 'Paki' house open, and disgorge upon them a ferocious horde. The surprise of the attack occasioned an immediate disorganised retreat. The skinheads took flight in every direction, the lucky ones tailed by a revolutionary, the unlucky by a relative. I found myself charging down an alley between two blocks of houses. I was pleasantly surprised that my victim was shorter than myself and even though he had a bomber jacket on, he didn't appear that bulky. He was a kid, I guessed about sixteen. I could easily keep up with his desperate flight. The alley opened out onto another terraced row of houses. I felt in command enough of the situation to consciously decide that even though he was a kid smaller than myself, he would get at least one substantial slap. I lashed out with my flat hand a hefty blow to the side of the head. The power and surprise of the blow from behind knocked him off his feet. He veered off the road, tripped on the gutter and went sprawling across the narrow pavement. His head went through the bars of a little picket fence, made from very light metal, and into the low privet hedge behind. He tried to withdraw, but the now bent steel on either side of his head prevented any escape. I looked around, and saw that we had been separated from all the others. I looked again at my victim on all fours with his head stuck in the fence. His silence was that of a mouse trying to pretend he isn't trapped under the sofa by a huge cat who has the whole night at his disposal. I was charged up to the eyeballs by a great infusion of adrenalin surging through my body. His undefended arse sticking up in the air was just too inviting. I took two strides and gave it my best shot with my stronger right foot. I noticed I was wearing my Doc Martens shoes, he his Doc Martens boots. At that moment it seemed to be the most fundamental difference between us. Screw age, politics, race, religion, origin, education… it was the footwear.

Now my mood changed from confidence and relief at being on top of the situation to a rage at the thought of this kid hurling rocks through the window of the Latif family where the baby slept. I bent down and shouted through the fence at my victim who was groaning an imitation death rattle. 'I should kick your fucking arse.' Given the events of the last few moments the absurdity of that expression changed my mood back from one of rage to one of good humour and I returned to the house.

My jubilant comrades, both relative and revolutionary, spoke of the beatings they had handed out. Comrade Vaughan P had not been a party to the successful defence against racism that night He had been last out of the house and his duffel coat had got caught on the gate latch and almost been ripped off his tiny frame. But he could still celebrate, as could the Latif family, who after months of suffering, had enjoyed one night of relief and revenge.

It was a rout, that night, but obviously something that could never be sustained, and a few weeks later, realising the impossibility of their situation, the Latifs moved to Dalston, back into the neighbourhood in which there were many other coloured folk like themselves. Back to the ghetto.

†††

Our weeks were filled with sales of the revolutionary propaganda at tube stations, political meetings which were numerous, and then on the weekends demonstrations and more demonstrations. It was the age of the political demonstration. As much as the Left was in its element, so was the Right. The National Front and the more right-wing British Movement were having a field day recruiting. Their campaigns against defenceless immigrants and vulnerable non-white Brits allied to football hooliganism were providing an exciting alternative to the deathly boredom of unemployment. They staged provocative demonstrations, usually about some race issue. One was to march through the streets of Shepherds Bush, a march for which permission had been sought and granted. The Left immediately mounted a counter demonstration and got permission to march near the route of that of the fascists. The organising committee could not agree on anything like slogans, tactics or conduct because of the sectarian nature of all of them, they could only agree that they would all be there. Saturday came and there was a huge turnout of Left support all assembled behind their various group banners and our motley crew that numbered in total about seventy comrades.

At one point in the march, down a side street it was possible to see the march of the fascists some blocks away. The police had cunningly directed both marches so that they wouldn't intersect at any point. The management of our group of seventy amongst the several thousand protesters, decided to defy the direction of the police, and drive a wedge through the thinnish blue line, thereby taking the rest of the following demonstrators straight into the path of the fascists. Word spread through our squad that this was the intention; the comrades formed themselves into a wedge and on a given signal drove at right angles to the march and through the police. All hell broke loose. The line of the police was temporarily breached; reinforcements came steaming in with batons flailing. Our small group was not followed by the thousands behind, so was isolated in standing combat with the police. I only remember a crush of bodies, fists and batons flailing before going down in a heap and then being yanked to my feet and frog-marched off to a police van waiting, no doubt, for just such a situation. The police van was divided into small cubicles, just big enough to house one inmate per cubicle. One by one, as all the other cubicles became occupied, the doors slammed shut. Then silence reigned except for the distant chants of 'Pakis out now' in my right ear and 'fascists out now' in my left, as the two demonstrations went on their separate ways.

We seemed to wait a long time after the noisy slogans had receded into silence, long enough for me to completely inspect my cab, its construction and material composition. And long enough to begin contemplating whether to try communicating with the other prisoners. Everyone was silent, only the occasional sound of material rustling as people moved informed me that the van was full. I felt a fart coming on, but to break the silence in such a way seemed somehow to diminish the cause for which we had just been heroically engaged and captured. Let alone what my fellow faceless inmates would think. After all, this was England, the land where people sedately place their knives and forks together on completion of a meal, where people stand in queues and say please and thank-you: one simply did not break wind in England. My attention again turned to the possibility of communication. Should I start tapping on the panel in front of my face, the noise of which would be about two inches from the ear of the inmate in the cubicle in front. What message should I tap out? Should I introduce myself first, or just keep it simple with a plain 'Hi?' Then two thoughts struck me simultaneously. Firstly, I didn't know any tapping language, neither finger nor foot, and secondly I wasn't Marie-Antoinette in the Tuilleries, or Nelson Mandela on Robben Island. My reveries were cut short by the sudden roaring to life of the van's engine. We were off, rolling and swaying this way and that. It only took a few minutes before we passed through a huge door, which slammed shut just as the engine again cut to silence.

Doors in the van were opening and the noises of feet told of inmates leaving the van. My door remained shut. The shuffling of feet subsided. A few doors slammed in the distance. Then silence. What was going on?

Had they forgotten me? Or was this a tactic to try and break me? I had to remind myself again that mine was more of a misdemeanour than a crime, and certainly, whatever it was it still had to be proved. I sat for two hours in that tiny space, at one point when I heard someone passing, I did start banging on the walls and shouting. Whoever it was called out 'Won't be long now.' Eventually I was released into a room adjoining all the cells and adjudged that they'd left me in the van because they'd run out of space in the cells. They were now 'processing' all those arrested. Several of my fellow comrades were waiting in the line.

First in the line was Paul S, a young working class lad in his first year of college. Second in line, incredibly, was the mother Sabine N, still managing to look regal and in control. The officer behind the desk took Paul's details down... name, address, next of kin, that sort of thing. When the questions finished he instructed Paul to go over to a second officer at another desk and have his fingerprints taken.

'Why must I have my fingerprints taken?' Paul S asked him defiantly, as any revolutionary worth his salt might be expected to.

'Because I say so,' said the policeman.

'But I'm not guilty of anything.'

'What are you doing in here if you're not guilty of anything? Just stop by for a burger and chips, then did we? Git.' said the copper. 'Now fuck off before I send your fingers over there without the rest of your body attached.'

Sabine N drew herself up to her full outraged height. This police officer was not only flouting the law but in threatening violence was thumbing his nose at the very heart of the democratic norms and conventions that were his job to protect. While Paul S was a working class kid who might understand street democratic procedures, she would protect his interests and that of society by approaching the matter at a higher level.

'Excuse me, officer,' she intervened, with her cross between Germanic and English snob accent… 'I demand to see the commander of this station, this is outrageous.'

'Oi, and who have we got here,' said the officer, 'the fucking queen of England. Well let me tell you something you don't seem to be aware of lady. This ain't Buckingham Palace you're in right now; it's the fucking slammer. My slammer. Now one more peep out of you and you'll feel my fist removing your teeth on route to ripping out those warbling tonsils of yours.'

That was the end of that matter.

For myself, I played the very co-operative naive foreigner, caught up in a sight-seeing trip that proved to be the wrong spot at the wrong time for a tourist. While that got me out of handing over my fingerprints it didn't stop me earning the little charge sheet, much like a parking ticket which at one point read: '…on Sunday 23rd November 1980 in a public place at Maida Vale W9. Did use threatening behaviour whereby a breach of the peace was likely to be occasioned.' Although the charge seemed a minor one it went on to explain that my behaviour had contravened three acts, sect 5(a) of the Public Order Act 1936 as amended, section 7 of the Race Relations Act 1965 and the Criminal Law Act of 1977. Up until this point I had been feeling like a bit of a Wally, but with all these acts contravened under my belt I felt I could eventually walk out of that station with my head held high.

Back at headquarters the arrest of about twenty comrades didn't so much as cause a ripple of thought, discussion or analysis. After all, look what happened to Trotsky when the Soviet secret police caught up with him in Mexico. Everyone was just preparing for the next day's early morning sales at the tube stations and markets. Obviously contravening three acts of bourgeois law in only one act of behaviour, and that behaviour was only threatened, not actual, could not be considered impressive. One shuddered to think how many acts one would contravene if one's behaviour were actual and not only threatened. Or maybe the British state itself would just crumble, not having enough acts in its arsenal to cover such an eventuality.

I remember little of my day, or should I rather say moment, in court. The policeman who collared me couldn't remember much detail but when I got my time in the box I not only overdid the tourist in the wrong place at wrong time thing, but went on to deliver a half-baked political speech which caused the prosecutor to sit down with a smug 'no more questions m'lord.' The judge brought his little gavel down on the bench pronouncing me guilty, fined me £70 and three months' sentence suspended for a year. Striking in the context of what was to follow, this was, by any stretch of the imagination, an inconsequential event in the day of that court. The inconsequence of the court matters of that day were such that they did not warrant the observance of a representative of the media, nor was the weather inclement enough for the public gallery to be used as vagrant shelter to London's less fortunate members of the public. In short, besides the direct participants in the case there was no one else in the court.

†††

At this time my father was a professor at the largest university in South Africa, the Witwatersrand University. He was a professor in the medical faculty, a chair having recently been created for his specialty – Ear, Nose and Throat. His father, my grandfather, as described earlier, had been one of the original South African white Communists, prominent in the trade unions. My father was born in 1917, the same year as the revolution in Russia. He was brought up by his father who was in and out of gaol and quite unable to bring home the bacon. From a very early age, my father had to fend for himself. It was indeed an achievement that he had gone through school, put himself through university and then sponsored his own specialization at the Royal School of Medicine in London under a prominent British specialist Sir Terence Cawthorn.

Now, at the time of my own revolutionary involvement, my parents were moving into the autumn years of their lives. My father was in semi-retirement. From very humble beginnings they had made a success out of their time on the planet, and successfully launched three children into a world in which they were already making a solid contribution. The fourth child, me, who they also believed to have been successfully launched, had suffered several rocket booster malfunctions, most of which had been concealed from them. This last child was about to come crashing back into their lives on earth in a most unfortunate fashion.

Four months after my conviction for threatening behaviour, an article appeared in a South African daily newspaper, which was headlined: 'SA man at anti-Nazi demo fined.' The article then went on to read: ' A South African arrested while trying to break through a police cordon during an anti-Nazi League march here last November, has received a year's suspended sentence and was told to pay R120 (&70) costs at the Marylebone magistrate's court. Johannesburg-born Timothy Haynes, an unemployed construction manager, denied using threatening behaviour at the march but was found guilty'.

This useful snippet of information was then syndicated to all the other papers, and the following day every daily paper in the major centres of South Africa carried the little piece. My parents happened to be on holiday at a coastal resort on the day the offending article was printed. They were in fact reclining on fold-up beach chairs, on golden sands and with the sound of the surf breezing through their ears, when my father opened the paper. Needless to say, their afternoon at the beach was spoilt, as was the rest of their holiday. My father had to come to terms with the fact that his son had gone the way of his own father, his great grandfather and his ancestor. He had spent a lifetime overcoming the impediments his early life had thrown at him, he had succeeded in becoming a model, a pillar of albeit an imperfect society. Just when he could sit back and enjoy the peace, security and happiness of that life's work… Life is not very sensitive or understanding.

The headline caught his attention: 'SA man at anti-Nazi demo…' and he had pondered what an anti-Nazi demo might be. Was there a resurfacing of the Nazi movement in England? Was this a euphemism for something else? And why would a SA man take an interest in that? The usual newspaper claptrap that wouldn't make sense at all.

But he read on because there just might be some answers to these questions. Then he got to the name. Timothy Haynes. It was his name. He was confused by shock for an instant. What was that name doing there in the paper, in that article? The blood drained from his face. He felt cold. He went back to the beginning and read the whole thing again, trying to make sense of it. The only words that made sense were… 'arrested… Timothy Haynes… Guilty.'

When he'd regained his mental composure, he passed the paper over to my mother knitting in the chair alongside his own. She was always sitting knitting in a chair alongside his own, only the scenery changed. Sometimes she was staring out at the garden at home, sometimes she would be staring out over the lake at their country retreat, now she was staring out at the sea.

'Have a look at this Ida,' he said. She set down her knitting on her knees and tilted her head back so that she could read through the bottom segment of her bifocals.

When she got to the Timothy Haynes, there was a sharp intake of breath and her top teeth clamped over her bottom lip. They both looked out to the sea. She then read the article a second time and passed the paper back to him. He re-read the article.

'What's he doing? Is he going to gaol?' my mother asked, confused.

'He's a hothead, just like my father,' my father said, 'all emotional response and no thought process.' He shook his head. 'And no responsibility.'

Silence again prevailed.

'He also knows how to ruin a good holiday,' said my father.

'Don!' my mother said, with an edge of reprimand.

'Well if it happened here, I might well have been able to call some people and organise something. But in London? I can hardly phone Sir Terence and ask him to intervene at the Home Office. And if I did, and he could assist, Timothy would probably call him a Nazi or something worse, we just don't know any more.'

'But is he going to gaol?' my mother asked again.

'It says it is a suspended sentence, but it is unclear how long the sentence is or the suspension. Of course if he breaks the law again before the suspension is complete then he will go straight to gaol. And if he's involved in all this political activity over there, the chances are that he will break the law again and go to gaol. I encouraged him to go overseas in the hope that he might leave politics behind, but it looks like he's in with another crowd of crackpots... or maybe it's the same crowd. Isn't it amazing how some people simply can't appreciate when they're better off than other people? No they must get down there and rough it with the common man, instead of rising above and using their skills to improve the world. Maybe he simply doesn't realise what he's getting himself into. I'll talk to him on the telephone when we get back home to Jo'burg.'

And phone me he did. The relevance of the fact that there was no reporter in the court on the day of my appearance lies in the article in the South African newspaper some months later. How did this come to be? At this particular phase in the political history of South Africa, both the internal and external security networks working for the preservation of Apartheid were well known. They pulled off some spectacular international stunts, for example the bombing of well known high-profile political figures in the resistance movement, and were suspected of the killing of the Swedish prime minister Olof Palme. The tapping of telephones of political opponents was therefore routine. In Britain, the IRA could not be defeated by the British State, which arguably ran the most sophisticated security service in the world. At the moment when my father was lifting the telephone to discuss my political affiliations, Margaret Thatcher was taking a particularly hard line with the imprisoned IRA hunger strikers. She was allowing them to die rather than concede any ground on the question of Northern Irish independence from Britain. Bobby Sands was about to die, the political temperature in Britain was high, and the security services no doubt working overtime to prevent any backlash.

This was the context into which my father phoned to express his concern at my political activity. Rightly or wrongly I was sure that the telephone was bugged by the security services of either South Africa or Britain and possibly both. Lastly, several months had passed since my misdemeanor, and the whole incident was completely out of my mind. I recognized his voice:

'Hi Dad, how are you?'

'Not too bad son, how are you?'

'Fine thanks. How's mum and everything there?' I asked.

'Fine thanks. But what's going on over there? What are you getting up to?'

'Ag, the usual, going to work. It's been a bit cold, and you know England, it can sometimes be a bit dark and gloomy.'

'No, I mean you were arrested, what was that all about?' His knowledge of the arrest took me by surprise.

'Oh that, but it was months ago. All forgotten about now.'

'But you were found guilty, and you've got a suspended sentence. How can you forget about that?'

'Well it was such a tiny stupid thing, not worth dwelling upon really.' I wanted to try and stop the conversation on this topic on this international line. But the more I tried, the more my father would have none of it.

'There are people dying for these causes. Do you want to be a martyr like Bobby Sands? And even as a supporter of the IRA you could go to jail forever,' my father said. If there were any listeners to this conversation I was now in the league of Bobby Sands and a staunch IRA supporter.

'Dad, this has got nothing to do with Bobby Sands and the IRA who I don't support anyway. I was protesting about racism in South Africa. Also I don't think we should have this conversation on this telephone right now.' I said desperately.

'I just want to let you know that Bobby Sands will die, and you will go to gaol and it won't make one jot of difference to the world at large. But your life will be ruined.'

†††

At the regular Sunday branch meeting of the tendency, the planned activities for each comrade were posted so that we all knew where and how we were to be employed. Of course there was no choice in the matter, we had effectively given over our lives in the pursuit of the revolution in much the same way as a Moony would Moon, or a follower of Sun-yat-sen would wear brightly coloured robes, cut off all his hair except for a little tail hanging down the back, and walk around the streets of London barefoot banging little bells and drums. Our appearance and activities were equally as unattractive to a normal person, but like these other weirdos we couldn't see it. Like them we were also too busy moving onto the next activity to ever get a chance to look in the mirror.

This week one activity posted for me was a little out of the ordinary. It simply read 'Brixton Town Hall – Wednesday 3 pm.' As instructed I arrived at the Brixton Town Hall at 3 pm, in my Nato parka and drooping hold-all filled with my unsold propaganda material. Another comrade whisked me away hurriedly, and instructed me to get rid of the bag. I was horrified.

'What?' I asked incredulously, 'aren't we selling the paper?'

'Are you nuts?' hissed my senior comrade, 'Sabine and Vaughan are getting married and you're about to give the whole game away to the bourgeois state.'

I quickly left the building and deposited the offending bag in the car of some arriving comrades. I then noticed that some of the comrades had doffed their caps, so to speak, or more precisely combed their hair on this auspicious occasion. An explanation is necessary before proceeding further.

Probably half the comrades in the organization were foreigners who had been recruited usually while on some student visa or other. They'd played out time in England to the maximum on the back of this device. Another mechanism had to be found to allow for further prolonged residence as the pursuit of revolution was a lifelong commitment. The institution of marriage might be a device for the exploitation of women, but in this case it could be used against the bourgeois state. So all the British comrades were instructed to marry the foreigners to prolong their residence. And a respectable number of comrades were instructed to attend in an attempt to give the affair a semblance of authenticity.

In this particular case, nothing could give the proceedings an air of authenticity. Sabine N, substantially taller than her fiancée, looking especially regal in a classy albeit understated black number was the diametric opposite of Vaughan P still in his tan three quarter coat with the little horn buttons. Thankfully, his hood was down. He'd brushed his red Prince Valiant mop as well as his Hush Puppy suede shoes.

Sabine N could not disguise her loathing at having to go through this indignity. Vaughan P was doing his best to make it look genuine, but there was enough pride left coursing through his veins for him to feel a little put out by her condescending attitude. The whole scene was so absurd that the council official could not but smell a rat. He too got into the spirit of the occasion by slipping in a couple of mischievous lines about the woman obeying her husband and then at the end asked the happy couple if they were not going to mark the glorious moment with a kiss.

Sabine N's face went scarlet, her ice blue eyes were sharp and angry enough to slice titanium, but she was caught. She turned and bending over planted a rapid kiss somewhere near Vaughan P's eye. He on the other hand was delighted at the prospect of kissing Sabine N. His chances of ever kissing anyone in his miserable life were slim, and here was Sabine N offered on a plate. He was going to enjoy this, but simply did not move fast enough before his eye was closed by her haste to get the job over and done with.

Then there was trouble at head office. A flutter of counter-revolution was in the air, and it didn't even come from the ranks of our counter-revolutionary underground cell. It came from a model candidate member. One of his tasks was to sweep the steps in the dingy and decrepit Brixton office. He raised the question why should he sweep the steps? Why should this task fall to the lot of the lowliest members of the organization? This was a Communist organization. Surely it was necessary for new members to be engaged for every available minute in education, education, education. Or rather re-education, re-education, re-education (as most of them were graduates, some with Ph.D's). It did seem a bit of a waste to have rocket scientists sweeping the steps. But then what was the answer? To hire an outside worker? No, according to the complainant, everyone should do the job. The carpenter, the rocket scientists AND the leading body. In that way all members would never lose sight of the lot of the worker, and always have in the forefront of his/her or her/his mind what exactly it was that we were there for. It was a classic. All hell broke loose.

The knives came out for the comrade who raised the question. His name was Dave D. A whispering campaign of discredit breezed up and down those dusty steps. Petit bourgeois idiot in need of more education was the most obvious and expected description of Comrade Dave D. Lazy white South African male used to having a maid do the sweeping for him was another. Cmde. Dave D was made the personal charge of a central committee member all to himself for intensive fast track re-educative care. Oh, and the steps sweeping roster was doubled to twice a day from just the once, both to be done by Dave D.

Dave D took his medicine with good grace. He was soon made to understand that degrees count for nothing in this microcosm of the New World that had been established. He obviously realised, or maybe had even been informed that if he had committed this misdemeanour at any time in the last six decades in another country, he would have died in the icy wastes of the steppes of Siberia, if not worse.

†††

One evening a carload of us were off to Wapping. Rupert Murdoch had just introduced new technology into the newspaper industry in England by setting up the first high tech newspaper production plant in Wapping. Of course it meant the elimination of many jobs from the old industry in Fleet Street forever. The big unions supported by the loony left were up in arms. Every night Murdoch's new shift went into work, the unions tried to prevent them. And the police had the job of preventing the lefties from disrupting the changes Rupert was making.

The rules of engagement between protesters and the establishment were just beginning to change. Up until then, a row of Bobbies in their ridiculous hats linked arms and shoved against the massed weight of the protesters. The Bobbies always won because the common sense arms linking technique gave them more strength with fewer men. The protesters never linked arms because half their argument was against the organization of the establishment, and the linking of arms would be a doffing of the cap to the state on that one. Secondly, although the protesters were linked by a certain commonality of program, in England this was not sufficient reason for people to start touching one another. By contrast, in South Africa all protest, all political expression, was and is held only by people dancing with each other en masse with such intensity that the original intent of the march/demo gets lost in a haze of other desires.

At Wapping, Bobbies with designer helmets, batons and long flowing capes came out on horses. They were certainly an intimidating sight.

Visions of Doctor Zhivago and that terrible massacre of the poor workers by the Cossacks on horseback with their sabres jumped into my head. In the mayhem of the jostling Wapping crowd romanticism had overtaken me. I was seeing Julie Christie, blond hair shining, red gown with bosom heaving about to be ravaged by that skunk Rod Steiger while her real love was receiving a cutting up from a flailing sabre out in the black-ice streets.

Someone was relating the story about how Sam Fox, the Sun newspaper's favourite page three girl with gigantic boobs, had broken the picket line the day before. During the day, when there was little movement of people in or out of the plant, the protesters had been enough to form only a small token presence at the gate. Sam Fox stepped out of a black cab and wobbled into the gate under the protective arm of some Bobbies. One of the workers shouted hopelessly, 'Sammy, don't do it, you're one of us!' Sammy was tottering along on impossibly high heels, about to enter the building. The worker shouted again 'Sammy… ' But before he finished his second plea, Sammy stopped and turned, almost losing her balance. It looked as though she was about to open her big fur coat and reveal page three, three-dimensionally in broad daylight.

'Sammy…' the worker croaked again, his whole being so fixated with what might be about to happen that his balls had clearly tensed up and choked his larynx.

But instead of opening up the coat, she had unfurled her small hand and blew a little kiss and smiled a big lipstick smile in imitation of the great Marilyn before disappearing into the building no doubt to discuss her next photo shoot.

†††

As the organization's carpenter I was invited to do work for the better-off comrades, and then their sisters and brothers and parents and friends outside the organization who had money. Which was awfully convenient for me: I was never unemployed.

After the incident at the old age home some comrades got together and decided that they had better learn some self defense as, given the direction top management were bent on heading, this incident certainly would not be the first and last time we would be under physical threat. Conveniently there was a karate teacher who held classes in Dalston, and when he heard of our work he was happy to supply some free tuition to the organization. Ten comrades without any major physical impediment were selected to undergo this training. I was one of the ten. So was a leading comrade, a woman named Fran E who was a bit of a skinhead herself. She had her hair cropped very short, and was a stout woman, in fact both her shape and her style was modelled on the macho skinhead chic. She and I had never had much to do with one another, she being in the upper echelons and me being on the ground.

The instructor was illustrating how to handle battle at close quarters. For example, what to do to defend oneself against someone who managed to get you into a headlock. In order to practise these manoeuvres we had to work in pairs, one to be the aggressor, the other to practise techniques of escape. Fran and I were paired up. While I never thought of myself as Mr. Macho, I was quite tall and had always done physical work and a bit of sport, so when it was my turn to put Fran into the headlock, no matter how hard she practised the techniques I held her tight. Of course this reflected badly on the techniques, it showed that unless people were vaguely physically similar, the techniques were hopeless. And I was in a terrible quandary. Because she was a senior comrade should I let her get out of the lock? If I didn't make out like she could escape easily would I be put on double early morning weekend sales at East Ham market? On the spur of the moment I decided to throw caution to the wind and face the consequences. After all, we weren't liberals, we were revolutionaries, so let me practise what the organization was preaching. I held her tight. She squirmed, she hit out with her elbow, she kicked at my legs, and she twisted and turned and at one point got her teeth into my arm but then thought better of it. I held tight.

That particular manoeuvre was finished and the class moved onto the next one. Now she did pull her rank to ensure that we were partners on this one as well. And we went through the same sequence of events, possibly with her trying even harder. Then I realised there was another dimension to this little charade between the two of us. The game seemed to be turning her on. Because of our respective positions in the organization this new situation was filled with a little excitement and tinged with fear. I felt rather like a small child being put in charge of a box of matches for the first time.

A couple of weeks later I was invited to her flat in my capacity as carpenter to erect some shelves for her burgeoning collection of books on the struggle. I never suspected a rat, for Fran E very carefully instructed me what she wanted doing as she was not going to be there, it was a working day and she had a good job in the media industry. It was with genuine naive surprise that I arrived with my toolbox and began following the elaborate plan to find the key and open the door, only to find the procedure unnecessary because Fran E opened the door for me. She was dressed only in a light see-through nightshirt.

She said she was unwell and had taken the day off work. She showed no interest in my being there and disappeared into her room leaving the bedroom door slightly ajar. I got on with the carpentry job.

At about eleven o'clock in the morning she came through to where I was busy. I stood up, screwdriver in one hand, wooden batten in the other. She put her arms around my neck and said something like 'oh, I feel so bad.' My mind went into confused overdrive. I didn't want to drop the screwdriver and wood, that would have been too noisy and dramatic. Should I lift her with my stiff-arms like a fork lift truck onto my newly erected shelf and begin pumping away? No… far too movie clichéd. Should I lift her gently through to her bedroom, lay her softly on the bed and twiddle, lick and gently jab away all through the day? No… Far too petit bourgeois decadent. Should I cane her bum with the wooden batten conveniently located in my hand and take it from there? No… Far too thermidor thirties for us modern revolutionaries. And last option, do nothing and see what happens next. She was the senior comrade and was in a leadership position anyway.

In the absence of being able to make up my mind on the above possibilities, I went for option four by default. After an uncomfortably long interval of nothing happening, I broke first. I squeezed her sides uncomfortably with my elbows and said 'do you want me to get a doctor?' She removed her arms and separated from me, looked me in the face with a combined expression of disappointment and contempt, turned around and disappeared into her room this time shutting the door firmly. Whatever was the right option, I'd clearly taken the wrong. And while the right option may or may not have given rise to fun times, it certainly would have stood me in good stead politically in the organization. With an ally in a position considerably advanced on that revolutionary ladder of which I was yet to feel my toes on the first rung, maybe I would have gone places. I let myself out of the flat at the end of the day without disturbing her. I don't recall whether or not I had the courage to charge her money for the day or not.

Meanwhile, on the other side of town, my live in 'partner' who had joined the organization at the same time as myself, had been similarly invited, nay instructed to visit another senior male member for some instruction on … guess what… imperialism. I admit and agree that imperialism is a difficult concept to grasp compared to its crude older brother colonialism, but one can't help thinking that its very nature was designed to snare the committed and unsuspecting into compromising positions rather than exploit less fortunate countries and continents. So she, the committed innocent paid another leading member a visit at his private residence, as ordered. He had been born into money, educated at the very best English schools and university and had a senior position at a very fashionable glossy publication. He was thoroughly bourgeois, he could have, he should have been spokesperson to Prince Charles. What the hell was he doing in the revolution?

And of course when my partner arrived at his London pile, his wife happened to be away on that very day. Cmde James W. set to work sitting obscenely close. The preferred teaching method was the old time honoured arm loosely draped around the back and thighs in close contact from knee to scrotum. And then followed the process of extrication and escape, which resulted in relief followed by fear, and disappointment followed by anger. Like mine, her revolutionary future was consigned to the dustbin of history. Cut short by sex, or lack of it.

I was very shortly to feel the chill wind of no friends in high places, and then the inevitable parting of the ways between the revolution and myself. Or should I say potential revolution, because history has come to reveal that the revolution's potential was never realised. There was nothing so much as even a tiny blip on the societal seismograph.

I had been operating as a 'candidate member' for two years without qualifying as just plain 'member'. I was still on probation as it were.

But I'd been around, shown some commitment, some loyalty, been kicked around a bit (actual and metaphorical), failed to show 'flair for theory', I was male (bad rating), I was white (worse rating), and I was ex-South African with accent (shocking rating). But, when all was said and done, given that the organization was not bursting at the seams with new members, I was useful for making up the numbers. Top management decided that they better give me some incentive for staying given that 'member' was not within my reach, so they promoted me to Propaganda Sales Organiser or PSO for the east London branch of the organization. The PSO was the stuff of ultimate humiliation. It was about getting poor and on the dole members to cough up for the rag they had sold on behalf of the organization and had long since spent on tube fare, a café breakfast or a quiet pint.

Come the branch meeting every Sunday, comrades would avoid the PSO like the plague. The PSO had to report to the branch meeting on the propaganda sales. I would make it my business to root out the leading members on that day, no matter what it took, and extract from them an explanation as to why their sales were so poor for that week. I would then report all the reasons to the Branch meeting with complete sarcasm and scorn, much to the hilarity of the other junior members. After a few weeks, the leading members who had come to understand the game, started playing their own game. PSO's report was the last slot of the meeting. So for all the items before PSO report, the leading members would do the same to me. This all started out as good-natured banter, but as the weeks went by and I persisted with my controversial PSO reports, their frustration grew simply because I had more on them than they had on me.

Then one Sunday morning when all comrades were usually out on selling excursions at markets, tubes, meetings, demos or rallies, I saw one of the head honchos returning from the corner café still in slippers with the Sunday papers tucked comfortably under her arm. Like most other 'normal' people in London, she was headed back to bed, to tuck up comfortably with the best read the bourgeois press had on offer. I saw her, she saw me. She knew she was in for big trouble that night at the branch meeting at the words of my PSO report.

She came to the meeting that night and saw me smugly waiting for the last item on the agenda, the PSO report. She had had the whole day to work out a way of escape from the horror of exposé that night. The meeting started and she called for an urgent item to be added to the agenda, which must be discussed first. The item: my indiscipline. She described how she had caught me reading the Sunday papers in the east London branch office when she had returned there to replenish her supplies of propaganda material which she had exhausted through some especially diligent sales activity. My PSO report that night was dull and boring. It was also my last. As putrid and pathetic as these organizations' politics and existence were, I understood for the first time, how people were killed within them. I could understand for the first time with perfect clarity how and why the gulags of Stalin accounted for the lives of millions of people.

The Revolutionary Communist tendency became the Revolutionary Communist Party. 'Living Marxism' was launched in 1988 as the journal of the RCP. The party collapsed but Living Marxism lived on as 'LMMagazine.' It closed in March 2000 following a lawsuit brought by ITN against an article claiming that the genocide of Bosnian Muslims did not happen in the camps of Srebronitsia.

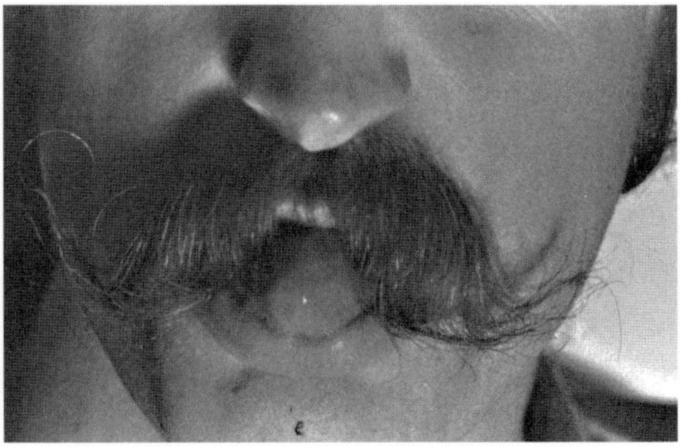

STORY 6

COMMUNIST HOLIDAY.

After two years of hell in the service of trying to make world revolution in a very left wing organization in London, I had resigned. Walked out, just like that. After the madness, the intensity, I couldn't have imagined it would be that easy. My time there had been extreme and exhausting. But now I could cross the line into space inhabited by *bourgeois* thoughts, and the first one that came to mind was in the folder labelled *'holiday'*. Before applying to the real world for re-integration into it, I needed a break. You don't just throw out a few years of being brainwashed to think in a certain kind of way just like that. But a holiday would certainly help.

I watched a few travel programmes on the TV and read the holiday ads in the papers, not really with enough enthusiasm to make it happen. Besides, I couldn't afford to go and plonk myself down on a white beach under a coconut tree in Mustique for a month or two. That seemed to be the bulk of what was on offer. So when a friend told me of a dirt cheap snow skiing holiday at travel agent Thomas Cook I was delighted. He then told me it was Bulgaria. But I've just escaped Communism, I yelled.

Skiing is skiing, who cares what colour the snow is, he replied. An image of the piste, the lycra gear, the sunglasses, the flying hair… I phoned agent Cook the next day and signed Clare, my partner, and I up for a week in Bulgaria. I shouldn't have.

The Bulgarian airways plane was old and tatty, as was the piece of meat thrown down during the flight. It was also the first time I noticed that most of the plastic bits that make up the insides of a plane are not really joined to the steel tube which is the outside. The plastic trim that frames the window sometimes did not line up properly with the window. If the plane was going up, you could see the steel of the shell under the glass, and if the plane was going down you could see the steel on top of the window. Did this happen on Lufthansa too? I persuaded myself that these were merely the observations of a Comrade, hypersensitive as a result of recent de-enlistment.

We landed at an airport attached to the second city of Bulgaria. Somebody told us the name of the town was Plovdiv. Everyone at the Plovdiv airport was dressed in some military getup, all as unfriendly as hell, not helped by the fact that only Bulgar was spoken and only Bulgar was written. Being a language using the Cyrillic alphabet, it was completely unintelligible. For example the word 'exit' looks like N3CO#. The entire tour party was ushered into a too-small-for-comfort room and the door was locked. There were insufficient chairs for the number of tourists, so people settled wherever they could. In true English fashion nothing was said, even though the turning of the key in the lock of the door was cause for a great deal of wonderment bordering on concern.

Most of the tour party consisted of couples. None of the couples knew each other, so it was like one big encounter group. One big silent encounter group with everybody determined not to be the first to speak. After the first half an hour there was some inter-couple exchanges, largely consisting of statements of necessity like 'I'm going to need the toilet soon.' After one hour a few people were beginning to crack. Was this the snow skiing tour? someone asked. Yes it was, came the reply.

Another half hour later someone addressed the whole party: did anyone know what was going on? No, nobody knew. Some bright spark got up and tried the locked door. Everyone watched. The door was locked. The bright spark had made an idiot of himself: he had to go the whole hog now. He compounded his own embarrassment by knocking on the door. The joker (in a crowd of thirty there's always a bright spark and a joker) said 'who's there' and a few people tittered. That seemed to break the ice a little, enough for the pragmatist to ask the generality 'are we going to sit here all night'.

A cynic enjoined with 'are we going to sit here all week?'

A circumferentially challenged woman with headgear similar to that worn by a Second World War pilot who we later came to know as Brenda said: 'we should knock down that bloody door! We've paid good money to be treated like this! We should demand our money back!'

'Sorry I can't offer this around' said the piss-cat, taking a bottle from his bag and swigging from the neck 'I've only got the one.'

'Would anyone like a mung bean whole-wheat sandwich,' offered a hippy looking girl sitting cross-legged on the floor and unpacking a little lunch pack directly onto the Plovdiv Aerodrome carpet.

Two hours were up and the room was humming with the sound of new found camaraderie born of this adversity. There was an indignant gathering on the one side of the room that was planning some sort of action. There was another section that were not going to allow a small thing like being locked in a room spoil their holidays, so they were whooping it up. There was already some antagonism between the two sections, the indignants believing that the good timers were not taking their plight seriously enough and possibly even jeopardizing their chances of early release from the room. The good timers were not going to be dictated to, either by the state of Bulgaria or by the indignants. A young man next to the piss-cat started objecting to the rapidity with which the alcohol was travelling out the neck of the bottle and down the neck of piss-cat. We discovered later that he was in fact the son of the piss-cat. He then laid a hand on the bottle and tried to wrestle it from the grip of the piss-cat. The piss-cat violently pulled away and in the process the bottle was inverted and a huge dollop of its precious cargo landed on the big new duvet skiing jacket of the gent next to him. He told the father and son to 'fuck off', the son got the bottle and the father lunged after it only for all to land in a heap on the floor. General mayhem ensued.

And as if this was all part of the plan, at that moment the door was opened and the dishevelled tourists all in a heap and feeling like a gang of petty criminals caught in the act, were escorted by some squat thick-necked communist Bulgar army men with short machine guns strapped across their midriffs out of Plovdiv International and onto the tourist coach.

The tour bus wound up narrow roads through a ravine, higher and higher up into the mountains. The party on the bus was subdued, tired and no-doubt contemplating the inauspicious start to the skiing holiday. Perhaps they were peering into the darkness through the windows of the coach and thinking to themselves that if the world outside was covered in snow it should surely be a bit lighter than it was.

Finally the twinkling lights of the resort came into view up ahead. The coach pulled off the road and onto a grand traffic circle. It then stopped at the foot of some wide steps leading to the hotel entrance. As the tourists alighted from the bus they were relieved to step into the remnants of some snow, some white and black slush that had been turned up by the wheels of the coach. We disgorged our luggage from the hold of the bus, and struggled under the weight of the bags up the steps – no assistance in sight. It was 10.30 p.m. Some workmen were hanging the front doors of the five-star hotel. And they were mightily pissed off at having to stand aside while paying guests of the hotel made their entrance. Or maybe they weren't pissed off. I came to understand during the next week that the disposition of all Bulgars was not a happy one, by standards of the Capitalist West that is. It is possible that they expressed happiness by ways other than smiling and laughing, but then these ways were not easy to discern. There was no-one else in the lobby. The tour party once again threw their bags in a heap, satisfied at least that this door could not be locked on them. Ten or twenty minutes went by and members of the tour party started drifting away, to look through the windows of a curio shop, to see if the place had a decent pub, to find someone who might tell us where to from here.

Eventually a Bulgar emerged from somewhere, looking like one of the army men at the airport *sans* weapon, expressing much annoyance that everyone wasn't there, in English tempered by much Cyrillic. While waiting for the others to return he gave as an introductory rather than welcoming speech. He explained that there were certain features of Bulgar custom which we would find different to our own and that both sides should exercise restraint and understanding in order to prevent any difficulties. The most important aspect of difference he had found in his years of conflict resolution was the yes/no conundrum. In Bulgaria yes was denoted by a shake of the head and no by a nod of the head, the opposite of our convention.

He then informed us that we should understand that finishing touches, like the hanging of doors, were still in process. We were then told which room numbers were ours (there weren't any keys yet) and we made our way upstairs. The rooms were standard hotel design, bathroom at the door leading onto room, double sliding glass doors onto small balcony. As we entered we were hit by a blast of air hotter than a sauna. I immediately opened the sliding doors on to the balcony from whence cold air came blasting in. I almost expected to see storm clouds form in the middle of the room and drop a shower on the bed. I searched for a thermostat. There wasn't one. So we cunningly left the balcony door open, placed the bed exactly in the middle between hot and cold and were very pleased to pull the duvet over our bodies on the cold side, leaving our heads in the hot. It was a difficult and delicate balancing act, but we managed to execute closure to that day and dreamed of skiing down mighty Bulgar slopes on the first day of the holidays.

Next morning we found a large eating hall, and faces that we recognized were scattered around the long eating tables. Some very unfriendly-looking Bulgars in white jackets and little towels thrown carelessly over the shoulder were bustling about doing breakfasty things. We pulled out a couple of chairs and sat down. One of the white jackets came over and said 'breakfast'; we said 'yes please,' nodding simultaneously. He retreated to where he had been previously standing. Another tour member sitting a couple of seats away was smiling.

'You nodded your head,' he said, laughing.

'Quite right,' I said, I had forgotten the speech on the different convention. I beckoned the waiter to return. He returned looking a bit sour, quite clearly he was not one to be beckoned with.

'Breakfast,' I said and shook my head.

''Breakfast?' he said and nodded his head. Now what was going on? Had he just remembered the difference convention and was making the adjustment? It was a fifty/fifty situation, with breakfast at stake.

'Breakfast,' I said, concurring with his nod by a nod of my own. He went back to his spot and stood still. I was wrong again. The neighbouring tour party member, who I recognized as the joker from the night before, gave a small cheer and laughing said to us:

'Now you're faced with a good news and bad news situation. First the bad news: if you call that guy back he'd sooner knock your block off than get you any breakfast. But the good news is the breakfast isn't worth looking at, let alone prodding with a spoon.'

'What about tea or coffee?' I asked.

'At the table over there, help yourself.'

We decided to give breakfast a miss. Giving the system a break, all of a sudden seemed like a good idea. Before coming down for breakfast we'd peered out from our balcony over a green pine-forested landscape. Only little wisps of snow still lay attached to branches, and piles of white in very protected places was all there was of snow. There would be no skiing today. The sky was blue which meant there was no chance of a fresh flake either.

We walked around the buildings of the resort. There was a tacky tourist shop that wasclosed. We looked through the glass at the merchandise, combination romantic Eastern European peasant-style Stalin art, not very attractive. We found an indoor pool that some of the waiters from breakfast were obviously freshening up in. The air was chemical acrid, the water was green, and didn't have the fluidity of water we were used to. Somehow it was more dense, more the quality of dribble than water. We decided against.

We left the buildings and decided to walk around the grounds. We walked through the still fir forest, swathes of which had been cut as tracks for skiing. Snow was in evidence. The trees were very lightly brushed in white, the swathes between were now patchy white with green showing through. The path we were on led to a ski-lift station. Some bleary-eyed operators of the station were looking busy, but clearly not expecting any call for their services. We continued on the path and came to a log lodge, a structure designed to look warm and inviting in a rather crass and obvious sort of way. The kind of place that might have appealed if one had been doing some logging in the wastes of Siberia and was just about to expire from cold, hunger and thirst. The real intention of the place was to get down-market Western European tourists pissed out of their heads as fast as possible, especially necessary when there was no snow and therefore nothing to do. And although it was no more than 10.00 a.m., the place was already rocking. Again we recognized several members of our tour party in conspiratorial groups around dingy tables.

We pressed on with our walk. We came to another lodge in another part of the woods. And then another. They were dotted all over the hills. We stopped in and had some coffee. The coffee was horrible: obviously they only made it as a special, the supposition being that by the time you needed coffee in this establishment you wouldn't be aware of the finer points, like taste. We hit the road once again, and found ourselves back at the bottom of the ski-lift. We bumped into another tour party couple, easily recognizable by the bright orange troll-type mops that both of them were sporting. In 1982 in England that headdress was quite funky; in 1982 in Bulgaria that headdress was positively dangerous. We said our hellos and discovered that they had just covered the same route as we had, and were equally as disheartened. Our first friends, lost souls thrown together by adversity.

The cable car now appeared to be functioning. Although there were no takers, the Bulgars in the station seemed to be putting it through its paces, oiling and greasing for busy days to come we imagined.

'Well, let's' just take a ride,' one of the parties suggested. We all agreed.

Our new friends strapped themselves into the first two-seater chair and were yanked off. Ten yards later Clare and I did the same. We were airborne, ascending the hill at the level of the top of the fir trees. Compared to everything else so far, it was fun. At the top of the hill we alighted, walked around the area from which we could imagine ourselves taking off, skis attached, on an awesome downhill, the pleasure of which was just a snowfall away.

Lunch time was approaching, so we returned to the platform and re-mounted the chair-lift. We didn't want to miss lunch, after all an incorrect nod of the head had caused us to miss breakfast and having lunch was an activity that would help to while away the day. Halfway down the return journey home, the cable came to a halt in mid-air. We were dangling fifteen metres from the ground.

At first we thought that the ski-lift had stopped to fill up more chairs, and that therefore we would proceed again in a moment. Ten minutes later were still all a-dangle. We began a dialogue with our new orange-haired chums in the next seat 10 metres further down the hill.

'Any idea what the delay might be?' we hollered.

'No idea. Maybe in this part of the world with everything under construction it's a power cut.' they hollered back. Another few minutes went by. It wasn't particularly cold sitting there. But there was now some cloud cover, the day had turned murky. We looked up and down the path cut through the trees for the ski lift. No sign of life. Only brambles, bush and patches of snow between the dense fir forest on either side. Neither the ski lift station from whence we had come or to which we were going was visible.

'Let's try shouting, maybe they forgot we were still in transit,' the orange heads called back up to us. With that we all started yelling, different things, alone, in unison. It was still quite fun, on holiday, dangling in the air, with some new friends. After all this little experience would be over in a minute, and what a good tale for one of those desperate lodges somewhere underneath. However, half an hour later, we were still sitting there. At three quarters of an hour with the murkiness of the day having intensified to the extent that one could begin to wonder whether it would be possible to survive a night up here or not, we entered a new dialogue with our fellow travelers.

'How far do you think it is to the ground?'

'Twelve, fifteen meters max,' came the reply.

'Could one of us drop?'

'That's four or five floors of a building.'

'But it looks quite soft down there, on a slope with snow and bush.'

'There might just be rock under that.'

All four of us went into silent contemplations. After a while someone shouted, 'People have survived when their parachutes failed to open.'

'People have died tripping on the front step.'

Clare was now weeping. It was the third time that day that she had wept. She wasn't usually the weeping type, and each of the weeps had been precipitated by different emotions. This one was a mixed bag of anger, of incredulity at having found herself in such a ludicrous situation when she was normally an adventurous but not foolhardy person, of frustration at being unable to do anything about it, and the beginnings of concern.

'If I hang from under this chair I can probably clip 3 metres off that drop,' I said, trying to be of some help. She howled a bit louder.

We had now been there more than an hour. This was absurd. If it was a mechanical breakdown one would have imagined some kind of drill to be in place to prevent this situation from occurring. I was now super-angry myself, and remembering those Bulgars at the airport and the hotel was cause for even more despair. Just as I had worked myself into a silent albeit motionless frenzy, the ski-lift cable ground back into motion and we resumed our journey down the mountain.

We alighted at the ski-lift station, and through the glass we could see the operators. We attempted to call them using hand signals and arm movements. They acted dumb and uninterested. They certainly weren't going to be summoned by some Western bourgeois scum tourists. Either that or, like the nodding/shaking of the head communication problem, hand and arm movements were also not as international as we Westerners would like to think. But then one of the Bulgars gave himself away. He made a signal with his hand. He looked at us and lifted his hand repeatedly to his mouth. Food. He was eating. His lunch? Yes, his lunch. He was telling us that the ski lift was turned off while he had his lunch. Oh, now how could we be so thoughtless? Of course, why didn't we think of it before we got on the ski lift at lunch time? Silly old us. We signalled our apologies, and went on our way suitably humbled.

By the time dinner time came around we were seriously hungry. We'd spent the balance of the afternoon in the hotel room. The bathroom was tiny, a small wash hand basin, toilet bowl and nozzle sticking out of the wall which was obviously the shower. No door. The spray washed over everything in the shower cupboard and the escape for the water when it finally landed on the floor was through a hole in the middle. And it was hot in there, even without the door. So emerging from the shower, gagging for air, one would dash across the room to stand in the cool from the open glass balcony doors. But we were finally ready for dinner.

And we were ready for the waiters. I was not going to lose another meal through too cavalier an attitude to the head nodding/shaking confusion. I would ignore these conventions completely and use some hand signals which I now knew to be international. The waiter sidled over to the table awaiting instruction, or rather, appeal. I lifted my hand repeatedly to my mouth and then added thumbs up. He looked at me with contempt, and then went into a nodding shaking head ritual accompanied by some obviously insulting verbals. But as Maggie Thatcher once said, admittedly about an altogether different matter, 'my head was not for turning.' I lifted my hand to my mouth, I rubbed my stomach, I gave him the thumbs up, I pointed backwards and forwards to Clare and myself. But I did not nod or shake my head. I hung in for all I was worth against his diversionary and intimidating tactics. Eventually he could see I was not going to be swayed, and he disappeared into the kitchen. Shortly afterwards, he returned with two plates which we assumed was the soup.

The soup was yellowish oil with some pools of reddish stuff which broke the surface tension in a few places, and a couple of tiny brown blocks which we assumed to be meat. The main course was the soup with slightly less oil, slightly more reddish stuff and some bigger blocks of meat. There was no vegetable, or fruit afterwards. We chewed on some old crusts which we dipped into the oil to soften up a bit and thus avoid breaking Clare's teeth or my plate.

Most of the other members of the tour party tucked in, but then most of the other members of the tour party were in the midst of hangovers from the early morning drinking in the log cabins. Except for the father and son team, who were clearly not bothering about the evening meal not on account of its poor quality, but because they were still arguing about the consumption of alcohol, an argument which once again erupted into violence right there over the dining room table. This time no-one batted an eyelid. They were just left to go into a clinch with each other on the floor. We went off to bed depressed and Clare had another little weep. That was four sets of tears on our first day of the holidays.

We were hoping to be woken in the night by a rush of snow blowing in through the open patio doors, but were disappointed to wake up the following morning with the rays of the sun shafting through the branches of the firs outside and settling on the bedclothes. However one shifted the bed-linen the patches of sunlight would simply rearrange in a different design. There was no getting rid of it. No single new flake of snow had fallen during the night, and without the dislodging of the sun no new flake would fall during the day. And it would take several trillion new flakes to make a ski possible.

Clare and I decided we should try to get away from the resort for a while. There was a second cable car which travelled to the top of a mountain in a different direction to the first. We looked carefully at our watches to ensure that we wouldn't be sitting on it through lunch or tea, and then quickly climbed aboard and we were off to the top. At the top of the mountain we alighted and noticed another lift which travelled down the other side of the same mountain, obviously to service another ski run when and if the snow ever happened. We boarded this one and alighted at the bottom of this slope. Close by the ski lift station was a public road which wound down into the depths of the valley below. One could just make out the roofs of a small town in the bottom of the valley. Clare and I decided to walk down into the town, have a look around and then find our way back via the road which we figured had to go back through the main ski resort.

The sun was shining, although it was cold, and cooling further as we descended into the valley. The road was not in good shape. The buildings on small holdings that we passed were old fashioned and poorly maintained. The odd farm machine or small truck passed us as we walked. They too looked old and decrepit.

The adventure to town was motivated by a desire to forget the holiday we were on. We would temporarily do this by escaping our holiday environment completely. This excursion was beginning to feel like a descent into hell and as such it was the cause of another type of depression setting in. By the time we got down into the bottom of the valley the surrounding mountains were high enough to cause the premature setting of the sun. The atmosphere was murky, the temperature freezing cold. Black snow and ice clogged up gutters, and in between the odd patch of white was mud.

This was the town of Momchilovtsi. The buildings of Momchilovtsi were bleak, even the new ones looked rickety. A walk up apartment block still under construction was scaffolded on the outside with rough bits of lumber lashed together with twine. Twine was obviously a valuable commodity in these parts. It performed a multitude of different functions. Besides its obvious usefulness in the building industry, the motor industry also appeared dependent on it. It attached exhaust pipes; boots and bonnets were held closed by it, and loads on roofs were secured with it. It held doors closed, it fastened number plates and bumpers. But most important of all, twine was all the rage as fashion accessory. It held up the torn pants of the men and holey skirts of the women, under which were thick dirty woollen stockings. It laced dilapidated old boots. It was used to fix the hair, to hold on the headdress and in some instances was just there in the middle of the thigh as worn by Geronimo the Apache Indian, or around the jacket encasing the bicep like Maradona the football legend.

I was reminded of Hieronymus Bosch (c.1450-1516). We were already floundering around hopelessly in his pessimistic, cynical view of life. We had descended into this town, this Momchilovtsi, like a descent into some subterranean settlement the inmates of which were the characters of his *Ecce Homo*. The painting represented the traditional belief at the time that ugliness and devilishness are identical. A ridiculous notion, but one for which Bosch could be excused as he lived before modern civilization. Here in Momchilovtsi, four and a half centuries after Bosch, it was difficult to believe that all these aesthetically challenged small town folk were nice people. Bosch's pessimism was so profound that scholars refused to take him at face value. Obviously none of them had visited Momchilovtsi.

Years later I read a travel/history written in 1853. Many chapters were devoted to Bulgaria, and one to the Rhodopes, the mountain range in the middle of which we were now located. In a serious investigation of 1853 the following observations of these mountain people were made… *'The frugality of this people is inconceivable, and they enjoy a singular vigour of temperament. A Bulgarian, on a journey will live for three weeks on the stock of bread and the bottle of raki he has taken with him, and he will carry home the whole of his earnings without expending a para… Such is his indifference to all the comforts of life that he does not even think of protecting himself in winter from the intense cold… Families are to be seen sleeping outside their cabins exposed to the cold winds of the autumn mornings, on the carpets that serve them for beds among the flowers of May!'* Whew! Life and death was tough. But in all societies, ancient and modern, so was tax… *'No species of property escapes taxation; if the Bulgarian has but a wife he must pay for the usufruct of that sole possession.'*

We were now completely depressed. We walked a few of the black ice-slushed streets, hands deep in fleece-lined pockets, shoulders hunched up against the cold, silent. Shops seemed not to exist. One glass fronted establishment with a single 20 watt bulb hanging in its belly had some decrepit steel shelves housing one item: what looked to be a big cake of sick-looking white cheese. The notion that there might be a place to get a drink or to buy a coffee was absurd.

And then we heard the crunch of many boots. We were close to a large public hall, and the army was marching into town and filing into the hall. Describing this rag-tag bunch of humans as 'the army' could only have been presumption, based on the number of different styles of army coat that they were wearing. Grey double breasted Swiss wool overcoats, East German trench coats, formal 'button to the neck' long brown Russian EM overcoats, German Captains' coats, fishtail parkas, West German NATO parkas, Light Field jackets, East German border guards' grey coats (some still sporting armbands), German BGS Rain Ponchos and American Civil war sack coats. Many had no coat at all and twine was once again everywhere in evidence. Clare and I watched this unhappy bunch trudge through the dirty snow and on into the hall.

'These must be the shock troops of the enemy Communism that we are threatened with by our leaders Mrs. Thatcher and Mr. Reagan,' I whispered to Clare behind my hand,' … the protectors of this little old town here and its precious way of life, and the greater Communist world beyond. Do you think they would gladly lay down their lives for all that we see around us?'

'If I was them I would gladly lay down my life right here and now for what we see around us,' said Clare. She'd had another cry and was now feeling a little perkier.

'Maybe that's why they all hang on to that twine. At a moment's notice, as it all gets too much, they can simply string themselves up.'

'That's fine for them. But what about us? How are we going to get out of this place? And we haven't even got any twine.'

'I certainly don't feel like trekking back up that hill in the cold and dark. I doubt whether that ski lift will be working by the time we get there. Let's get back to where we saw that bus station. Any bus driving that road will get us close to the resort.'

In the middle of town there was indeed a place where a bus stood. A bus that had come down the hill, turned around in the black slushy ice and looked as though it was pointed back up ready for a return journey. Its lights were on and its engine was stuttering. There was a tiny glass and tin kiosk just large enough for a single bag lady to be sitting within, and she was. We watched as a man approached the kiosk, offered some cash through the slot in the glass, the kiosk woman slipped him a piece of paper and he went and sat on the bus. I went to the front of the bus to see if it might reveal its intended destination. There was a sign with Cyrillic writing, it read Q\O^~/X. We approached the kiosk. The kiosk woman was stout, gray clothes, gray hair, stubby dirty hands, black nails, everything held together with twine. Was this a sole species of property over which some poor individual was paying a usufruct tax? No, that was pre-Communist. Clearly the unhappy expression on this woman's face told us that the entire Communist state had a usufruct over her unfortunate self. We said the word bus, we pointed at the bus, we said the word Pamporovo (the name of the ski-resort), we showed her some money and made as if we were offering it to her, we pointed at the bus, we made a hand signal like a bus going up a hill, made a low farting noise like the stuttering of the bus, put a thumb up and offered her money again. Nothing. Nothing that we said or did elicited the slightest response from her. She stared at us, with a mixture of distaste, contempt, boredom, non-understanding, disinterest, unwillingness, unhelpfulness, in short complete vacuum. Maybe she'd just died… The engine stuttering moved up a gear, so we hurriedly pushed open the battered door, and found a seat half way down the grubby aisle. There were very few people on the bus, with much the same expression as the woman at the ticket kiosk.

Much to our relief, the bus began a laboured journey up the hill we had come down earlier that day. After travelling for fifteen minutes the driver shouted something from his cab. Everybody on the bus seemed to enliven a little with this piece of action. Then he shouted again, and a definite buzz went through the passengers. The third time he shouted it was obvious that he was shouting at us. He then started banging the little shelf at the entrance to his cab. We assumed this was a ticket or money call. I took out some stinkis (the name of this denomination of currency - I kid not) which I translated into an ample sufficiency for the journey, and clambered forward to his cab holding onto the poles and straps while he was negotiating the sharp bends of the mountain pass. I placed the money down on his little shelf, a note and some coins. He looked up at me, he looked down at the money. He slapped the money off his counter roaring at the same time. The note disappeared down the steps, the coins clattered down onto the floor of the bus under the seats. This was obviously not the way to pay for a bus ride. But we had no way of knowing what the way to pay for a bus ride was. I returned to my seat not feeling sheepish or embarrassed, rather pissed off that everyone seemed so permanently pissed off. It seemed to be a universal Bulgar state. One thing was for sure, we were staying on that bus until we wanted to get off. Clare and I spent the rest of the ride speculating on the reason for this behavior. We came up with the following explanation. We should have paid the woman in the kiosk for a ticket. Paying the bus driver cash was a temptation to corruption. He had to make a song and dance out of it to show the other passengers how incorruptible he was, because no doubt all the passengers were possible undercover cops. It all made for beautiful, harmonious and loving social relations.

We saw the twinkling lights of the ski resort come into view, thankfully the incorruptible let us off the bus. To be relieved to be back at the resort was a new feeling in the downward spiral of bizarre feelings.

If you ever find yourselves sitting round with a group of friends discussing the possibility of a holiday in a small, off the beaten track mountain hamlet and the name Momchilovtsi comes up, be very definite in your response, a loud 'are you !XMM^o!?P mad!'

Unfortunately, we are not finished yet. We woke up the next day, broken people. Littered throughout the history of Bulgaria are people killed and maimed, sometimes in their tens of thousands, but never broken. In 1014 Emperor Basil Bulgaroctonos, (I'm not joking) the dinosaur of Bulgar history, defeated the incumbent Tsar Samuil's army and promptly blinded 14,000 prisoners taken. In 1205, Tsar Kaloyan or 'John the Handsome' razed Plovdiv to the ground and flayed its leading citizens alive. His nickname was changed to 'John the dog'. In 1240 Mongol hordes, fresh from their campaigns in Central Europe, desolated the entire country on their way home. Half of the Bulgarian population was massacred as they were defeated by Turkey and pulled into the Ottoman Empire. Every time the Turkish armies were beaten by Bulgaria's more powerful European neighbours popular rebellions against Ottoman rule flared up only to be brutally suppressed. Careful and exhaustive preparations for a final rebellion against the Ottoman Empire culminated in the April Rising of 1876. Bulgarian heroism was met with Ottoman savagery and the putting to the sword of 29,000 Bulgarians.

Somehow the Bulgars were always backing the wrong horse when it came to big power battles. The fact of their geographic position, a buffer between two great empires in the battles between European civilization and Oriental despotism, between Christian and Mohammedan religions, was most unfortunate. One would have thought that under these circumstances the best policy would have been to keep their heads below the ramparts, but not a bit of it.

At the beginning of WW1 they saw a chance to grab a bit of Macedonia, and after 3 years of agony in the trenches and mountains of Macedonia, countless thousand Bulgarian corpses were left behind in their lonely, defeated march homeward. And so it went on, until they found themselves a satellite of the Soviet Union, after unfortunately backing Hitler and the

Germans in WW2. Stalinism took control. As in the Soviet Union, the nation was paralyzed by police terror. Ten ministers, six Politburo members and 92,000 were arrested, dismissed or executed in the purges of 1949. Dealing with one's own internal opposition is one thing, but Todor Zhikov, dictator for 35 years, took the Stalinist struggle beyond the borders of tiny Bulgaria. Georgi Markov, a dissident writer living in London, was killed in 1978 after being stabbed by a poison tipped umbrella on London's Waterloo Bridge. The Bulgarian state security was also credited with a plot to kill the Pope in 1981, something not even the Soviet Union wanted to be associated with. These are only the highlights of their 1300 year history, a history of blood and guts, but very few breakages.

We woke up the next day on auto pilot, brains numb. We went down to breakfast. A tour had been arranged for the day. We would board the tourist coach, and take a ride down to Plovdiv. But first, having negotiated the windy potholed road down the ravine filled with old car tyres and used plastic bags, we stopped at the very famous Bachkovo Monastery. They weren't too pleased to see us. A small iron plated door reluctantly let us in, and we walked around the different buildings, chapels, cells, cloisters, ossuaries. Not a lot of life in the place. The day was overcast, it was dark, gloomy and cold. There was no warmth in that old monastery. The frescoes described what fate might be awaiting the sinners amongst us. Just like those paintings and sculptures in a million little churches in the France, Italy and Spain. One could imagine getting down to some serious sinning closer to the Mediterranean, but in Bulgaria? Nah. And then after being flayed alive by Mongol hordes, blinded by disreputable Tsars, skewered by Turks, poisoned by Stalinists… after all that… you get these people in funny hats, big beards, and black dresses telling you about your sins and what's in store for you on the other side. There was simply no place to hide in Bulgaria.

In one of the chapels a bunch of big beards had taken to an admittedly beautiful double bassed Byzantine chant. The coach load of out of sorts tourists traipsed into the small chapel and stood wheezing through the frankincense and myrrh smoking out of the swinging censers. And then… POP! Somebody had the temerity to fire a camera flash at the proceedings. The big beards were incensed, so to speak. The head honcho cut the vocals with a slicing movement of his hands, and scanned the tourist party with narrow eyes and glowing, angry pupils. The flash was such a shock that its source could not be immediately located. The head honcho moved into our tour party which opened a pathway in whichever direction it looked like he was going. He was searching out the culprit. As soon as the tour party realized this was a kind of witch hunt, they started closing ranks. Even if they thought the flash a foolhardy and inappropriate action, they were certainly not going to give up one of their own. The English are like that. Now they stood firm against the foreigner intruding into their ranks. Their actions fell just short of a jostle. Short of body-searching the entire party, there was no way the offending camera was going to be located and with a rumble of frustrated anguish that welled up somewhere within the big black tent he was wearing, he gave up the hunt. His party of supporters also looked anguished and hurt for their leader. Once again humanity had let them down; here was just another in a long line of similar disappointments. With a contemptuous flurry they disappeared through a low monastic door and were gone. The tour party looked a little sheepish but smirked back onto the coach happy in their small but tangible victory. The English are like that, it's one of their attractive qualities.

And we were off to Plovdiv. We emerged from the mountains of the central Rhodopes onto the Plains of Thrace at a town called Asenovgrad. The bread basket of Eastern Europe someone said. The clouds were now gone, the watery sun was making little headway through a duvet of brown pollution. In 1958 Comrade Zhivkov announced a Big Leap forward: Bulgaria's version of the 5 year Plan. Small towns and villages were bulldozed to the ground, and apartment towns like Asenovgrad built as the workers' new accommodation. The smallholdings were pooled into 3290 collective farms. This was it. The place was dead. It had no soul. And, worst of all, it didn't even improve production. It was one thing reading about this sort of thing on a piece of paper, quite another seeing the reality. Quick, move on. Fortunately the coach driver agreed and the bus speeded up.

And finally, Plovdiv. It used to be called Philippopolis, named after Philip II of Macedonia, the father of the great Alexander. On assuming power from the early death of his father at the age of 21, Alexander got the hell out of there and never returned. The Turks sensibly got rid of the popolis and renamed it Philibe. Then somehow, I couldn't find the explanation, it became plain old Plovdiv.

A guy called Lucian the Greek called Plovdiv 'the biggest and most beautiful of all towns' - in Thrace. By that qualification Lucian gave himself away as someone who hadn't travelled much. Today in Plovdiv there are Thracian fortifications, which were utilized by Macedonian masons, overlaid with Byzantine walls, mixed in with great timber-framed mansions erected during the Bulgarian renaissance. These used to look down on the Ottoman mosques and artisans' dwellings of the lower town.

Civilization then burrowed underneath all this antiquity in the form of a massive motorway tunnel, and most of the top was covered with Communist concrete and sleazy bars. But if you were into antiquarianism and had come armed with a strong magnifying glass and a large Kango hammer, you could penetrate either side of this concrete sandwich and find the history. For me viewing some tacky old broken down Roman columns sitting astride a four lane motorway tunnel rather disturbs the mental ramblings that antiquities should have the ability to invoke. It's rather like the modern trend in television imaging, where somewhere on the screen there is a moving picture; across the bottom moves the written word unrelated to the image; down one side are the latest statistics of something or other and the commentary has got nothing to do with any of it. And the human being for whose benefit this is being offered is vegetable-ised as a result. It is all so much, it is nothing at all.

When lunchtime came around we were all ushered into a restuaranty kind of thing. I wasn't really in the mood. I couldn't describe where it was, but it was another drab, pre-Communist upmarket big hall, obviously serving several different functions. It had an elevated stage, with ancient threadbare scarlet curtains and drapes. It had massive wooden exposed beams and ornate wooden windows falling apart from age and no maintenance. It was obviously a turn of the century plush palace: one could imagine old Franz Ferdinand himself doing a little quadrille down here before he unfortunately started WW1. An old man was playing a cello on the stage, his hair was long, white and greasy, his face pinched and drawn, his eyes sunken in sadness, his black suit and tails worn for as long as he was old. The hall was furnished with six tables and chairs each seating forty people. A rotund master of ceremonies showed our party to one of the tables. He too wore black coat and tails but he had altogether more energy than the musician. This was his show, if one could put it that way in a Communist country. He was very determined on what the seating arrangement should be, and placed everyone where he thought they should go, irrespective of his patrons' opinions on the matter. The results were husbands, wives, boyfriends, girlfriends, lovers separated, the brawling father and son team together, etc. Clare and I were the last to be seated. But we hit a snag. The table seated forty people, but there were forty-one tourists. The Communist version of musical chairs had left one person standing - me. I grabbed a chair from an adjoining table, and signaled to the people at the table to move up. The patron grabbed the chair from my hand and replaced it at the other table, wagging his other finger in my face and saying 'ne, ne,' which we'd come to understand as no, no. He then held the chair away from the second table motioning me to be seated. Forty people at one table and me alone at the other. I said 'ne, ne' in perfect Bulgar and grabbed another chair but didn't get it anywhere near the other table before he had the other side of it. It was a tug of war. I was outraged and determined not to have my lunch alone; he was beside himself with anger at having his instructions challenged. The tour party was getting into these scenes, so there was general approval for this incident, once again breaking up the boring day. He was bigger and stronger than I and he ripped the chair from my grip. I stood there and waited for the next move. He had work to do, forty-one people to feed. I was on holiday. We stood there glowering at each other, the cellist had reached the apex of a crescendo in *adagio*, before moving to *allegretto.* He hadn't seen any excitement like this for forty years. I still waited. Our podgy patron had to go off and organize the oil soup. He moved away and every five feet turned around to check my movements.

As he disappeared into the kitchen door, the tour party kindly made a space and I placed a seat in their midst. If the podgy patron wanted me alone at the other table he was now going to have to move me in a seated position on the chair. Minutes later he re-emerged from the kitchen and scanned the table for the enemy. Spotting me he grimaced in turmoil and pain. Turmoil because he wanted to come over and incarcerate me directly in the nearest gulag, but he had lunch to serve to forty-one people. Pain at having to live out the rest of his life thinking that someone had escaped obeying his instruction in his domain. The cellist was still spritely moving along in a fine ditty before an admonishing glance from the patron turned him back into a terrible *adagio.*

God, the holiday was nearly over. We just had to get through this lunch, get out of Plovdiv, a last night at the ski-resort, and then jet out of there in the morning. I could see it stretched out before me, it was just a question of knuckling down and going through the motions. Time didn't matter anymore. Just concentrate on the next activity. Don't lose focus on the final objective. Get out of there and be able to say, the holiday is over. The following day it came to be.

I'd tried working for Communism and holidaying in it. For me, both were a failure. There had to be another way to live this life. A new thought struck me. Why not accept the world as it was, warts and all, and simply try and make a way in it?

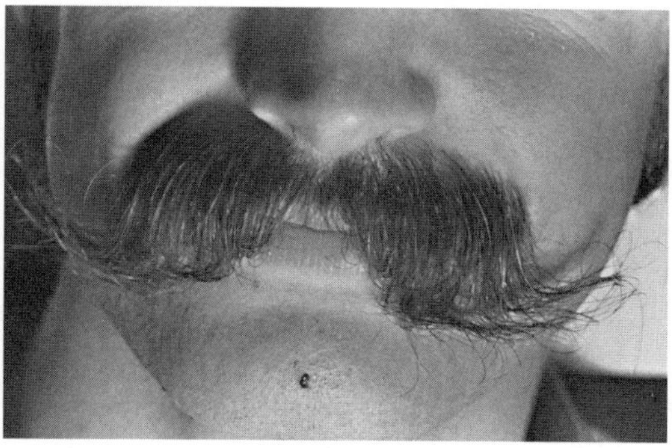

STORY 7

RETURN TO THE REAL WORLD AS WE KNOW IT.

I was born with a silver spoon in my mouth. I had missed the Second World War, I was white, I was South African and my father was a professional. He was a medical surgeon, which meant hard work, some extra money made and invested to make more. Not being a professional money man, it meant he lost his excess cash. By the time I was old enough to have used it, it was gone. Not that I wanted any of it, even it had been there. I had rejected the notion of materialism, I had rejected the idea of superiority by race or class, and believed the world needed a serious shake up. Hence the move from Johannesburg to London in the late 1970s. Hence the joining of the Revolutionary Communist Tendency. It was a nightmare, and after a very long and hard two years I threw in the revolutionary towel. A few years later the real communists agreed, brought down the Berlin wall and closed up the Communist shop. But even my silly involvement was not without consequences.

On leaving the Communists, I had to turn my thoughts to important topics such as how I was going to make a living and survive in the real world as it was, not a world I wanted it to be. The problem was that all the people who had provided me with gainful employment were attached to the comrades and the movement.

The challenge was compounded by my name change. I had become Comrade Simon Peters. I was Simon Peters to the outside world; in fact I had become Simon Peters to myself. So to start with, Simon Peters had to go and I had to return to my old self. There followed a good few months when I would bump into, or receive calls from people some who called me Simon, and some who called me Tim. I had to let Simon die a natural death. I couldn't say to people 'hey you know that Simon thing, it's off, just call me Tim.' But for some time I didn't know who I was going to be from one minute to the next. It was a kind of inverse schizophrenia. To the outside world I was two completely separate people. But to myself I was just the one guy. The worst of it was when I introduced myself to new people and I'd say 'I'm … ah … ah… ' before making up my mind who I was. While that was quite weird for me, it was even more peculiar for the people I was addressing.

Being in a political tendency was much like being in a religious order. Once you are exorcised, your whole life threatens to collapse. The god of the order has gone, friends have gone, work is disrupted, the social formation on which you had come to depend no longer exists; in short every aspect of life is turned on its head. And that is how these organisations and institutions operate, your whole existence becomes beholden to them and then they trade on the fear of leaving and the facing of nothingness outside of them. After my excommunication, I was visited by a senior comrade who asked me what I was going to do. She managed to make her question sound like a threat.

My old friend from Finsbury Park tube station, the person responsible for putting me on the revolutionary road, also phoned. I didn't know if he had been instructed to, or where his loyalties lay, but we met in the West End anyway.

'Why did you leave?' he asked.

'The lies, the deceptions, the dishonesty, the lack of any democracy even of a revolutionary nature, the lack of humanity, the personal ambition, the power trips... I lost the confidence that this could go anywhere... I lost confidence that even if it went somewhere it would be an improvement on what we've already got.'

'You realise of course that these are all *petit bourgeois* concerns,' he said.

'Fuck you, arsehole,' I said and left.

Christopher Hitchins once said: 'You do not forget, even if you come from a free and humorous society, the first time that you are with unsmiling seriousness called a 'counter revolutionary'.

†††

Twenty-five years later I was sent a YouTube tape of this same gent addressing a conference. Post his revolutionary life he had become a big shot in France Telecom. They called him 'Doctor'. I watched him waffling on, my emotions high with irritation and contempt. For while I was not able to break my *petit bourgeois* shackles, quite clearly he had managed to jump clean over that *petit* hurdle and was wallowing deep in the warm belly of the *bourgeois*.

†††

It was a cold nothingness outside of the revolutionary home that I was now facing. Fear and nothingness in a capitalist country. I had no capital, and I was totally unemployable. My CV showed a job in France picking grapes, but this wasn't the season, or France. When the picking grapes money had run out some years earlier, I had gone to an industrial employment agency in Kings Cross and taken temporary employment cleaning the toilets in a steel distributor's factory. It was temporary because the regular man was on leave. There was an upside. I discovered on my first day at work that I was not to be the toilet cleaner at all.

Toilet cleaning in Great Britain was not a job that one could just walk into. First there was the proper qualification, and then there was the experience. I was confronted with the truth of my pathetic situation. I had never properly cleaned a bog in my life. Sure, I'd dabbled in a bit of bowl cleaning. We all have. I had once lived in a London squat with a phantom bog stainer. Whatever time of the day or night that one chose to go to the bog, there was the stain in the bowl that needed cleaning. It always seemed to be there. Years later my partner and I met one of the residents of that particular commune and by way of finally exorcising the terrible experience of the phantom bog stainer from our lives, we spoke about it at our little reunion. We realised afterwards , gauging from the reaction of our old friend, that it was she who was the phantom bog stainer. We have subsequently lived in a state of mortification at our foolhardy openness. And needless to say, we never saw her again. We both have, on odd occasions, and in different locations throughout the world, come across a stained bowl and wondered if our old friend could have passed through just before us, as she was also a seasoned traveller.

If the truth be told (and it wasn't to the agent who interviewed me at the industrial employment agency) I'd never done the real job in my life. So it was entirely right and just that I shouldn't just walk in as the head bog man, I was only to be the assistant toilet cleaner. In those days the Brits were sticklers for this sort of qualification thing. I'm told it's even worse today. One cannot do the most menial of tasks without some company man demanding to see your ticket.

So my job was downgraded to holding the bucket, and then making it available to the qualified bog man. The qualified bog man, my boss, was a Polish fascist, a pathetically thin man whose stock outfit was tight black leather pants, pointy black leather boots with a chain and a greasy ducktail hairdo. He assumed that because I came from South Africa I would be interested in assisting with his plans to systematically eradicate all blacks from Britain. And when we had accomplished that job, he suggested we could do the same in South Africa. Some white people were trying to do that as we spoke, I told him.

I saw out my three weeks, and I'm sure the experience stood me in good stead. And seeing the last of those thunder-boxes, as they are known in India to the very few who have them, was as nothing compared to the joy of leaving the Pole behind.

The last item on my CV showed I had been a milkman in Brixton, mainly doing the council housing estates. I worked 7 mornings a week, starting at 4.30 am, for an outfit called RACS. If I recall, this stood for the Royal Association of Milk Canister Services. It was not quite the job as depicted in the Monty Python sketches, nude women taking in the milkman as well as their milk. Thinking back, there was one woman who did invite me into her flat, or not so much as invited but demanded, hollering from somewhere inside, that I should deliver the pint right to her hand. I followed the sound of the demand into the bowels of the ground floor council flat. It was musty in there, it was dank, it was full of stuff, and where a wall was visible it was damp to chest height. What air there was, stank of rot. With all windows sealed, the humidity was like the coastal tropics. She was sitting in the middle of the crowded space on what looked like a wheelchair with a blanket covering her legs. She was in pain, she was in distress, she asked me to help her. She pulled away the blanket from her legs. They were elephantine, and covered in sores and eczema and white paste. A fresh waft of rotting flesh found my nostrils. She proceeded to tell me how the social services had let her down; they promised to fix her flat, they promised to fix her, but here she was, her arm resting on the phone, cradling it as if it was her lifeline. Why don't you phone the council, I said? Why don't you phone for an ambulance, I said? They cut the phone off last week, she said. I'll tell them back at the yard, I said pathetically. I couldn't think what else to do. I told them back at the yard. The supervisor said that old geezer had been like that for years, always caught the new man on the job. I had some nightmares of that image, compartmentalized in my mind in the section entitled 'life in Britain'.

It took me six months of working everyday from 4.30 am in the morning before I was exhausted, and during the same six months I realised that the milk distribution business wasn't going to be the Monty Python sketch. Margaret Thatcher, the milk snatcher, first took it away from school kids, and then during her tenure presided over the demise of this service as well.

†††

Clearly what's been described above does not a convincing CV make. With no capital and unattractive as an employee, I was left to fashion something together out of my own resources. I had existed in the organization as a carpenter, a handyman. I figured every single building in London required maintenance. I just had to let the people of London know. So I put an advert in the employment wanted section of Time Out magazine. There was one call. Roger from Chelsea. He was having trouble with some cupboards he recently bought. I arranged to meet him and his cupboards. Gay Roger turned out to be very pleasant; his cupboards had recently been acid dipped, which was all the rage at that time, as an antidote to anything that had paint on it. The cupboards were split and warped into an unworkable, ugly mess. Roger and I sat down over coffee; neither of us was in much of a rush. He'd recently broken up with his boyfriend and was feeling down. His good-for-nothing-except-firewood cupboards hadn't assisted with his mood. My company and sympathy for his situation were some light relief. By the end of it all I spent a few days doing odds and sods around the house, re-hanging doors, servicing locks, a little shelf for the telephone, hooks hung all over the house, a leak in the roof plugged. And both of us were a little sad when there was absolutely nothing left that I could do, me not being gay and all. He said to me on parting that a friend of his would give me a call, she needed a reliable man. By the way, he said, she was a lady. Did he mean

'I'm a lady' in the 'Little England' sense of the expression? I wasn't sure what he meant but it didn't seem important. I simply needed some work.

To my surprise and delight his lady friend did indeed call. Her accent was posh but informal, as was her name – Toni. I figured that would probably be part of Antonia, especially if she was indeed a lady and not an ordinary woman. Lady Antonia, I imagined that sounded right. The address of the abode to which I was summoned was a high-rise block on the Thames, ninth floor, just down from Vauxhall Bridge. Not a very fashionable or picturesque part of the city at ground level in those days. It was dark as I emerged from the tube and walked the gloomy road parallel to the river Thames. I thought I was in the wrong place because the building looked like an office building. The foyer housed a door-cum-security man behind a reception desk. I told him who I was looking for, expecting him to send me on to some other address but no, there were two penthouse flats on the upper floors of the building. He called up to confirm my appointment. I was expected. I was beginning to get a sense of something out of the ordinary, certainly not something one might expect as a consequence of a single ad in Time Out magazine. My nervousness rose with the elevator. Having got this far, failure was not an option. I knocked on the heavy oak door, determined to act as though meeting these people was an everyday occurrence. 'Toni' answered the door.

'Hi' she said, with total enthusiasm. 'You must be Tim, come in.'

Small, slim, skirt, casual shirt, boyish hair, bright eyes and face, immediately likeable. Her legs ended in striped socks but no shoes. Depending on what I was to be asked to do, I would be busking big time on my capabilities. I had done a fair amount of busking in my short life to date, enough to know that every detail of every situation was part of life's learning curve that had to be remembered. No shoes were just such a detail. No shoes suggested that she preferred informality, that even though we were discussing business, it wasn't such serious business that shoes were required. Certainly not from her side anyway. No shoes further told of intimate association with this place, but I was soon to learn that that intimate association was not of a conventional variety.

The hall was black and white checkered marble floor tiles, dark oak skirtings and doors, white walls, down-lighters onto a set of Miró paintings lining three sides. Through the hall was the main body of the flat: an open plan dining area with Mackintosh table and chairs, and another huge area with soft living furnishings. But the overwhelming aspect of this immense space was the floor to ceiling glass windows on three sides. We were above the low buildings of Westminster; it was dark outside and it seemed as though the lights of the whole of London were twinkling into the apartment. The effect was stunning, it was breathtaking.

'Stunning,' I said. 'Breathtaking,' I added. A compliment always assists the process of endearment in the heart of a prospective employer. The compliment on the view was genuine.

'Yes, it is rather,' Toni said standing next to me and also looking out, 'but one does tend to get blasé about it.'

'And who would imagine such places even exist in London, it's easy to think of London as a drab city.'

'Well, even up here it sometimes can be a bit dull and grey during the day. But every night it's rather like those lights bring a little Christmas into our lives,' she said dreamily.

The phone rang. Toni jerked back into gear and took off across the huge expanse of open plan, skating in her socks across the shiny white ash parquet floor and round into an area furnished with a huge, modern light walnut desk.

'Oh hello Horace,' she said, 'he's just out the shower, I'll call him.' She dropped the receiver and came charging back across the ash field. 'Won't be a min,' she said to me as she skidded round the corner into the hall to call 'him'.

I had a chance to catch my breath and have an uninhibited look around. A few upmarket glossy books on the low table, an original painting on every piece of wall that wasn't glass window, fresh flowers. I was just getting to some leather bound books on a side table when Toni was back. She came running back round the corner and slid to a halt. Then she was off again. She ran everywhere in the apartment. She was like the cartoon roadrunner. But her energy was genuinely attractive, not irritating as it could easily have been.

I was left again to soak in the view. Given the squat we were living in at the time, this was as though I'd ascended into the clouds for a brief recuperative tonic. Before long I'd be descending in that lift back to ground level existence. After my revolutionary life, and then my revolutionary holiday, I was being given an insight into how nice it was up there with the three per cent. In the belly of the bourgeois. The phrase rang through my head. It wasn't half warm and comfy. My problem was the very temporary nature of my visit.

Toni was back again, with 'him' trailing after her at brisk walk in white toweling dressing gown and leather slippers. A short man, with open, sharp but pleasant features.

'Tim… Godfrey,' she sang out.

'Hello,' he imitated her sing-song voice, 'did you give Tim some champers, Toni?'

'Coming up,' she called.

'Bit slow tonight aren't we? Fix me one too, darling,' he instructed. His addressing Toni as 'Darling' was curious. Were they married? Very chummy if they weren't. He was now shouting into the phone.

'Horace? Horace, old boy… what's up? Did you fix me that box for Lords tomorrow … No?… What do you mean no, Horace? You run the whole damn city, but you can't get me into a cricket ground. Really, Horace. Call me when you have it organized… no excuses now Horace, I'm relying on you. Byeee.' Again delivered in singing voice mode.

'Tim,' he shouted, 'how's your cupboards, I need cupboards, can you do them? Toni, where's that champagne. If Horace doesn't get those tickets for tomorrow I'll have his bloody backside for breakfast. Tim, I need cupboards. Follow me I say.' He took off back through the hall with me in tow. He was clearly a man with no time to waste. Down the passage which was like a continuation of the art gallery hall, down-lighters onto pictures covering the walls.

'John Barry used to live here, and this was his music room. Born Free. Remember that? We need to turn it into a guest bedroom,' he was talking as we walked. We entered the room, all the walls of which were covered in shelves with dividers for LP records. There were thousands of them.

'Get the picture?' he said. 'Now I want cupboards to match the style of the flat, so they must match the cupboards in my room.' And off we marched to his room. The room was enormous, centre-pieced by the largest bed I'd seen to date. The floor to ceiling glass of the living area was now replaced with heavy floor to ceiling curtains which kept London out of his bedchamber. He walked me into his dressing rooms. The cupboards were solid oak stained dark with intricate panelling and recessed fretwork. 'And the insides…' he said, opening the doors revealing drawers, hanging space, panelled in oak or lined in felt and raw silk. He walked down the narrow passage opening all the doors on both sides as if reminding himself of the contents. The cupboards were full. At the end he said: 'Got the picture?' Of what I wasn't sure. How much clothing he had? Of what kind of fellow he was? What sort of cupboards he wanted?

'Simply replicate what you have here,' I said, to say something.

'Got it in one, old fellow! And as soon as you're done, I can do a bit more shopping.' He laughed at his own little idea.

'Well, yes, you'll have to,' I said. 'I wouldn't be bold enough to make the cupboards AND fill them with clothes.' This attempt at humour was a little risqué for this early stage in our relationship, but fortunately he was up for it and laughed.

'No don't,' he said. 'I don't want to be seen at the next Lord Mayor's Ball in an outfit chosen my foreign carpenter.' Now it was my turn to laugh. A definite breaking of the ice between us.

On the return journey back to the living room, Godfrey stopped in the hallway to point out the Miró paintings.

'Did you notice these originals?' he asked me directly, emphasizing the word 'originals'.

I wasn't sure what the intention of the question was. But I was relieved that I recognised them as Miró. On a trip to Spain some years before, Miró had been the flavour of the time in that country and I had seen his work in several places. And fortunately, I remembered some of the facts of the great painter.

'Miró?' I said.

'Yes... clever boy,' he interjected.

'...considered by some to be the greatest exponent of Surrealism. For others his curvilinear designs were too fluid for the much more geometric tendency of the surrealists.' My partner was an enthusiastic painter, I still wasn't sure where this gem came from.

'No, no, not that,' said Godfrey with irritation at having to wait to say his much more exciting piece. 'What do you think I paid for the set?' Back down on the street the comrades who had an artistic bent would be debating the curvilinear designs, here in the belly of the bourgeois, the cleverness of the artwork, although responsible for its monetary value, had been lost. As pearls cast before swine. Marx would have said something about the absence of culture of the bourgeois.

'Phew, I wouldn't have a clue...' said I.

'Guess - just... have... a... guess.' he said, rolling his eyes.

'Well...' I said, trying to think what would be the most circumspect answer to maintain my own dignity, and keep him happy. It had to be higher than he paid but not absurdly high. But I genuinely had no idea.

'Guess!' he commanded again with impatience.

'Twenty thousand pounds,' I guessed.

'Fifteen thousand,' he said triumphantly, snapping his fingers and walking into the living room.

'Wow,' I said without meaning. I had got it right enough to keep him happy.

Toni, who had been waiting patiently with a little tray with the champers had overheard the conversation in the hall. 'Where did that set come from again, Godfrey?'

'You remember old Jolyon at Sothebys, I met him at the club just when he was down on his luck and needed to do something urgently. These paintings came up and I helped him out of a tight spot. Lucky old me.' I was beginning to suspect that a lot of Godfrey's good fortune might well come about as a result of someone else's misfortune.

I sat down in that glorious living area above the lights of London and sipped the glass of champagne. But it was obvious that the business end of the evening was over. Godfrey had decided I was okay. The formalities, like money, would be sorted out by Toni at a later date without having to take up more of Godfrey's precious time. After all, time was money, and in Godfrey's case, time was a lot of money. So I was shown the door in the nicest possible way but without having finished my champers. I descended in that elevator, and disappeared into the cold, drizzle and dark of London. Back to our squat in Mile End, a terraced row that was shortly due for demolition, with dirty blue walls, dim lights, rotting wooden floors, rats scurrying underneath them, and of course the obligatory leaking roof somehow always managing to be above the bed. But I was feeling elated. In two easy steps I had hit a kind of a jackpot; it felt like another reward for leaving the revolution behind.

Clare met me at the door. 'Where's your motorbike,' she asked.

'I didn't take it because I was already on that side of town,' I said.

'No, I mean, where is it now?'

I'd left it parked outside the house on the pavement. I always meant to chain it to the fence but never got around to doing it. Now it was gone.

'Oh, shit.' I said, returning to the pavement and looking at the spot where the bike had stood. My elation of a minute before was now slapped down and replaced with dejection. I pointlessly looked up and down the dark road. I returned to the front door of the house, now closed on account of the cold weather.

'I suppose if I'm stupid enough to leave it unlocked some rat will take up the invitation to have a ride. I better go down to the station and report it.' I said to Clare.

†††

Commercial Road police station was a short walk away, so I set out through the dark East End streets on foot. I swung left at Locksley Street at the bottom of Mile End Park. Park was a bit of a misnomer; it was just some land that had been bombed in the war and never levelled out thereafter. The proposed demolition of our terraced row would be just a further extension of this piece of land. Although 'demolition' was too active a word to describe what was necessary to bring those houses down. Time and neglect had already done half the job. They were long since not fit for human habitation. The street lights were dim, and only every other light was still battling against the enveloping darkness. The self same lights, viewed from another trajectory, transported a little Christmas into the apartments of those lucky enough to live above this mess.

†††

Then out of the darkness came the sound of crunching feet. All marching in perfect time, like soldiers. The bodies were still in darkness, but slowly a squad of people emerged into the light. Dim light glistening off skin shiny from sweat. The noise was from the 'bovver' boots. Dark pants and braces. T-shirts emblazoned with union jacks. More huge union jacks on flags. All fat, with rolls of flesh like pink pigs. Heads shaven bald, the huge necks enveloping the chins and ending in pin-heads. It was a squad of fifteen or twenty young skinheads marching in formation up the road. They were under the light now. Arms out in front like the brown-shirts, legs straight. It was frightening and disgusting. I stood in the gateway of a house while they passed. Were they on an immigrant bashing mission? They were certainly making an unambiguous statement about who it was that ruled these streets. They passed by, into the light of another working bulb, and then on into darkness and finally the crunching receded into silence further down the street.

I shivered and resumed my walk to the police station. Turned right into Mile End Road, a major thoroughfare, but still in eerie darkness caused by the shadows of huge trees. Nearing Commercial Road the dim lights of the Chinese Take Away came into view. Then the laundromat with a down-and-out taking some rest inside, a minicabs 'headquarters' next door, and of course, the tiny Indian corner shop. All protected from the road by a row of bus stop shelters. Outside the minicabs shop stood a middle aged woman puffing vigorously on a fag, a heavy hold-all weighing her down. Under the bus shelter was a man. He was in a huddle with another figure. As I got closer I unconsciously noted that the two were in a grope, but then I become aware that the woman was very small. Then I realised that it was not a woman at all, it was a boy, a young boy. I was looking quite intently at the man and boy, and they noticed me coming closer and staring. They separated irritably. I was looking for a sign that the boy might be distressed but there was none. Only irritation. Then I heard the woman puffing on the fag: 'What the fuck are you looking at?' she leered, and I realised it was at me. I picked up my gait and hurried through the gauntlet. I crossed the busy Commercial Road, wondering if a responsible adult is supposed or expected to do anything about such a scene. Unable to answer my own question, I realised how inadequately equipped I was for life in the real world. For all of a second I yearned to be Simon Peters again. Simon Peters only had to blink and all the comrades would give answers to all the questions. Tim Haynes had to think for himself, he was on his own. I was relieved that it was only another hundred yards to the safety and security of the local police station. Maybe I should report this child molestation as well as the stolen motorbike.

†††

Painted in a messy scrawl across a wall of brown grey London brickwork were the words Isle of Dogs. What a name. But on this evening it was entirely appropriate. The horseshoe of land in the Thames, still far from the mainstream of London town, was yet to be discovered as a developers' paradise and renamed Canary Wharf.

The small satellite police station seemed deserted, the presence of the flag alone deemed sufficient to proclaim the maintenance of law and order. It was more a symbol of ownership than a police station able to provide a useful service. The entryway was the size of a shop-front, a counter stretched across with a hatch door closing off the front section.

I called 'hello,' to see if someone could be raised from behind the screen. A Bobby made his way from behind the screen to the counter. I told him I wanted to report the theft of a motorbike. While he was rummaging around unenthusiastically for the correct form to be filled out, there was a commotion at the door. A crowd of boisterous young people barged into the station.

In general terms, male and female were indistinguishable. Their gear spanned at least four centuries of fashion and style. There was the lily-white blond English with Mad Magazine freckles and only one front tooth. There was the yellow one with slit eyes and straight black umbrella hair. There was the blue black one with head scarf out of the top of which stuck the uncontrolled Jimi Hendrix afro. There was the brown one with pirate bandanna speaking in the queen's scous. And so on and so on. This was the new age, alive and functioning on the Isle of Dogs. While the motley crew seemed in party mode, it was obvious that they'd arrived at the satellite station on a specific mission. Some of the gang set up a little dance routine to the sounds pumping from a massive ghetto blaster supported on the rounded back of one of their number. Others started hitting on the lone police officer for some incident that had happened between the horde and the state earlier in the day. They had come to clarify the situation. The justness of the case of the horde was backed by strength of their vocalization of the issue, they were now screaming at the lone police officer who was totally overwhelmed. The horde was working itself up into an angry frenzy expressed through the medium of shouted lyrics and dance at the injustice they felt they had suffered.

If I understood the lyrics and the body language correctly, their complaint was that earlier in the day there was a fracas at a fairground in Victoria Park, and the police had arrested one of their number. The horde believed this person was at that very moment held captive in that station.

The inadequate and increasingly nervous response of the police officer was emboldening the crowd who were now beating with their fists and making as if to go over the thin partition. The escalation of the in-house frenzy was given added impetus by a shout from the bowels of the station from the comrade confirming that he was indeed still banged up there. Then a midget arrived. He was lifted onto the counter and promptly waved his comrades over.

I was jammed up against the wall of the station, feeling aggrieved that this bunch had pushed in front of the queue. This was Britain, a country in which the queue and everything it stood for, was sacrosanct. But however strong my feeling of grievance, it was overwhelmed by another impulse: that it would be far more expedient for me to shut the fuck up and get the hell out of there. Which I did. I fast jogged all the way home, past the molesting couple in the bus shelter, past the fascist brigade that was now returning from their mission. I heard police sirens in the distance.

Obviously the panic buttons had been pushed and reinforcements were rushing to the Commercial Road satellite Station.

I pushed through the front door, slamming it behind me, and holding it closed with my back while I caught my breath. Then I called, 'Hi darling, I'm home.'

†††

I made sure my clothes were right for an image of the clever craftsman for my first day of work at the great man Bowman's apartment. The middle classes love that kind of thing. I knew nothing of these subtleties before I came to London. On arrival I had called an old friend of mine, Matthew Parrott. He had been working as a painter and decorator for some years in London and knew his way around building a relationship with the client. He had just started the renovation of a complete flat in Knightsbridge, behind Harrods. The client was an English business consultant who worked mostly in Paris.

While the English businessman worked away in Paris, a whole gang of Matthew's family, friends and now me, had moved into the flat while the works were in progress. It was in the days of the orange people – disciples of Bhagwan 'the embodiment of God' Shree Rajneesh, or Chandra Jain to his family back in India. Indeed Matthew's girlfriend was one such disciple. Her orange name was Gooha, which I thought entirely inappropriate for a sweet girl from Essex who looked more like a Jane. It seemed as though no matter what segment of the social spectrum one subscribed to in those days, changing one's name was all the rage. Whether it was my good self in the Revolutionary Communist movement becoming Simon Peters, or Jane Smith from Essex becoming Gooha in the Orange movement, it was happening everywhere.

Gooha had turned the Knightsbridge flat's main bedroom into an orange temple: all dark, thick maroon velvets, beads, bells and the sweet stench of incense/hashish/Old Holborn combo burning on the dressing-table-cum-altar. As a mark of respect to his girlfriend's belief Matthew's wardrobe was also strong on the colour orange. Although wardrobe was too big a description for the sarong that he wore continuously. Underneath the sarong was nothing, no boxers, no Y-fronts, no thong, nothing at all. One of the most important tenets of Bhagwan orange philosophy was freedom of expression in all matters sexual. There simply wasn't the time to be messing about with items of apparel when one needed to get down and dirty.

Matthew's brother Stephen, also employed on the job and resident in the flat, had another small job that he had to attend to early in the mornings. He had to take the dogs of the famous English actor, Albert Finney, for a walk in Hyde Park every day. It was a decade in which relationships were important and relationships were not only those which happened between people. Relationships between anything and anything else were important. It was a time in which an American entrepreneur made a fortune out of selling rocks that one could get close to in a spiritual sense. So it was entirely unexceptional when Stephen developed a close relationship with Albert Finney's pooches. And every morning, before work started, over a gigantic English greasy breakfast cooked in the Knightsbridge kitchen, we would hear how things were going with the doggies. For some reason this chit-chat invariably set Gooha off, for before the story was even finished, Gooha and Matthew had made for the room, his sarong blowing off in the wind of the headlong flight, even though the tent-pole was quite erect.

One can imagine that with this much fun being had by all, not a lot of decorating work was going on in the Knightsbridge flat. In fact the most that had happened was the whole place had been stripped and scrapped. Debris and dust were everywhere; furniture had been piled into the middle of the room, half covered, half sat-on, all except the all important hi-fi which brought the soothing sounds of Frank Zappa, Captain Beefheart,

The Bonzo Dog Doo Da Band, Half Man Half Biscuit et al to life. Loud and continuous. Oh, and Keith Jarrett…

One morning breakfast had just been consumed. The greasy plates piled high in the kitchen, the smell of bacon temporarily overcoming the hash/incense wafting from the ashtray in the temporary ashram. Clothes and bedclothes strewn over every place uncluttered by decorating debris. Gooha had found some orange blooms which she was teasing into her unkempt locks. Stephen was just putting his hash spliff together. I had my feet up on the table with the morning paper. Matthew was in the bath. There was a knock on the door.

I seemed the least engaged at that moment so I went to deal with it. On opening I was confronted by a splendid lady, a woman of perhaps sixty-five dressed expensive but relaxed. Completing the ensemble was a wide brimmed hat at a jaunty angle, made lopsided by what looked like a bunch of wild exotic orchids.

'Hello,' she said, sticking out her hand. 'I'm Michael Phull's mother.'

I recognized the name as the owner of the flat.

'He asked me if I wouldn't mind looking in and seeing how you're getting on.'

My heart sank, probably because in its terror it forgot to beat.

'Yes, yes, please come in, hi, I'm Tim, I'm Matthew's assistant… things looking a bit scruffy at the moment… you know… all the stripping… Matthew… just in the loo… MATTHEW!' I shouted desperately, although the bathroom being quite close to the hall he had probably heard our visitor and was furiously throwing himself together.

'Certainly is a mess,' said Mrs.Phull senior as she strode into the belly of the flat. 'I never realised that silly boy of mine had taken on such a huge project. He told me it was just a dab of paint, I wonder if he has any idea what we have here. I should call him right away, he should be in his office at this very moment. Won't you get me the phone, dear boy?'

'Mrs. Phull!' Matthew made his entrance in pressed blue denim dungarees with a pasting brush and stripping knife just visible out of the top pocket, the blue collar version of a white handkerchief from the breast pocket of a dress suit.

'Mrs. Phull, how are you?' he glided across the room and clasped her hand in the two of his. 'I'm so glad you're not Michael, he wouldn't understand my needing to drop a bomb on his place before we can knock it into shape. Can I bore you with the samples? This is the paper we are using, raw Chinese silk, don't you think Michael chose well, a perfect match to his beautiful curtains…' And he was off.

I left the room, I needed to be out of there, the pressure was too much. Stephen and Gooha were holed up in the dark maroon bedroom. I joined them. Stephen was obviously feeling as concerned as I was at this turn of events. Not so Gooha. She wanted to go forth and meet Mrs.Phull senior, believing that any and all humans should be persuaded of the superior philosophy of the guru Bhagwan Shree Rajneesh. Stephen and I managed to persuade her that leaving the room would not be in the best interests of the entire group, and that any persuading that needed to be done, either in the field of lifestyle or works progress, should be left in Matthew's capable hands.

Half an hour later, we heard the sounds of the piano being played in the living area. I had to see what this was all about so I left our bunker. The covers had been lifted back off some of the furniture. Mrs.Phull was comfortably propped into a Versailles wingback chair alongside the piano; Matthew was playing. On the side table by her chair were the remains of a cappuccino that Matthew had ordered up from the new Italian coffee shop just opened on the street below.

He was an accomplished musician, and they were involved in a comparative discussion of Bach and Mozart, and he was illustrating his line of argument by playing snatches of various pieces on the piano. A change of tempo was required so he mentioned Keith Jarrett, who happened to be on tour playing at the Barbican that very week and being a jazz buff she was impressed that Matthew was not some stodgy old classical fart. He casually mentioned that Jarrett's Concert for Cologne had never been written down – transcribed was the word he used – but that he had taken it on as a project in his artistic time. And then…

'Matthew, you wicked boy, you've done it again. Just look at the time. I ought to know better by now. Whenever I come to see you, you make me so terribly late. And I'll certainly be reporting you to Michael, you naughty man. All this splendid work. Who says London's drab compared to Paris?'

With that she wafted out of the flat. Matthew closed the door and leaned his back against it, releasing a huge breath with a winning smile on his face. We all emerged to give him a standing ovation. Matthew was my mentor.

I considered I had been well schooled by Matthew in the art of employee-client relationships. Here I was arriving to work at Mr. Godfrey Bowman wearing the self-same denim dungarees that Matthew had saved the day in. 'Self-same' is not merely a figure of speech. These were in fact the same dungarees. It happened like this. Matthew came to find the weather and big city of London depressing, and headed for the States, where he landed in Oregon. He travelled light in those days, as we all did. Any possessions surplus to the barest of necessity were offloaded before moving on. I became the recipient of a large bag of his goods to do with whatever I saw fit. In the bag was some decorating gear, the brush, the Stanley knife etc… and neatly folded over the tools was the denim dungarees. They fitted me like a glove.

†††

I was met at the door by Mr. Bowman himself; not usually was he to be engaged in door opening of any description, but on this occasion he happened to be passing the entrance just as the bell sounded. He was in his same white toweling bathrobe and slippers with GB embroidered on the front in Monotype Corsiva style lettering. His entire head was smeared in a white paste.

'Good morning,' he said jovially. An amused look must have crossed my face.

'I can see what you're thinking,' he responded to my look. 'Well, let me tell you the reason I have this stuff on my head, is to avoid going the same way as you.'

It was true that the hair on my own head was thinning, and I confess to having thought very little about reversing the process. Of course, whenever an advert came up on the TV, showing a bald man on the one side, a particularly hairy species of ape on the other and a jar of hair grower in the middle, one was tempted momentarily to rush out, purchase the jar and get looking like the chimpanzee as soon as possible. But somehow laziness, scepticism or both seemed to intervene and the trip to the chemist was never made. In the case of coconut oil, while I could understand the logic – that coconuts have hair on them – I have never seen a coconut either with thick enough hair or a style that convinced me that its oil could really do the job effectively.

I never voiced these thoughts to Mr. Bowman. And I have also to admit that years later, like now, I am as bald as a coot, while I saw Mr. Bowman on the TV being carted off to gaol back in the UK and he had a great head of hair. So much for my theories on coconut oil and chimps.

'Now you know where the kitchen is,' Godfrey continued. 'Make yourself a cup of tea or coffee or whatever you might find there, whenever you need it. I'm afraid I can't be of more assistance than that, on account of my never having made a cup of tea or coffee in my life. But I'm sure everything's there. Maria runs a good and tight ship for me.' Mrs. Maria de Diaz was the Portuguese maid, whose ancestor might well have been the famed Bartholomew, the great seaman who got to South Africa first amongst Europeans. His shipping expertise had obviously been handed down to Maria.

†††

And so my work for the great man in the fabulous flat began. I was going to be there for several weeks, as besides the construction of the new cupboards in the spare room, other maintenance items cropped up along the way and my time in the flat was extended. While I laboured away on this task and that, I couldn't help being a part of what was going on in the flat. I had no complaint. After all, I was fascinated to observe exactly how the other half lived in London, especially as until recently I had been a paid up working member of The Revolutionary Communist Tendency, dedicated to the ridding of society of the bourgeois, the vermin I was now directly employed by. And I still lived in a squat in Mile End.

So when a champagne luncheon was held I got to take a peek at who was there and what went on. After all, as a big shot in the Conservative Party, and Maggie just come to power, Godfrey's guest list would always be dominated by politicians. But there were also the sportsmen, including some members of the South African cricket and rugby fraternity. This was at a time when there were no sporting links between South Africa and the outside world. And there was nothing funny about the whispered conversation between our man and a famous comedian, very popular on the circuit at the time, renowned for his pro-working class lefty albeit Scottish humour. The bottom line appeared to be money, because wealth brings power. Godfrey, however much he pretended to the contrary, had not been born into aristocratic England and aristocratic England does not easily accept pretenders. But with Margaret Thatcher in power, the pretenders were enabled to take advantage of all sorts of opportunities, not previously afforded. It was the epoch of the Bowman philosophy. An epoch in which, for example, ideas about the value of art were reduced exclusively to the bottom line – how much it was worth.

It wasn't long before his interest in painting surfaced once again. I was detailed to rub down and re-varnish the skirting boards in the living area which were, in Godfrey's eyes, looking a little shabby. The location of

Godfrey's desk in the nook of the L-shaped open plan room meant I was privy to his telephone conversations. Not that that bothered Godfrey at all. As far as he was concerned, I was all but lost in the hugeness of the tenth floor space above the Thames and London. Besides disappearing in the space, my station in the world measured 'low life' on the social Richter scale; Godfrey's outlook was that I was of such insignificance that my knowledge of his affairs would be of little consequence.

What I heard from Godfrey on the phone back in '83, down on my knees, rubbing the skirting, requires a sentence of historical context. In 1979, after nearly 40 years as the Shah of Iran, Mohammed Reza was deposed by a combo of religious leaders, some bourgeois and students. The monarchy was replaced by a fundamentalist Islamic republic inspired by the Ayatollah Khomeini. The first years of the new state were chaotic, and all sorts of racketeers and opportunists took advantage of the chaos to personally enrich themselves. The telephone conversation went like this:

'Hello Massoud,' said Godfrey.

...

'Fine, fine – have you had any luck yet?'

...

'What do you mean, difficulties? We're running out of time, and I'm running out of patience.'

...

'That's your problem, it's got nothing to do with me and I'm certainly not getting mixed up in it.'

...

'Look, you offered me some paintings, I've told you I'll take whatever you can get. I can't see what the problem is, it's not like they will miss all that decadent Western garbage. They'll probably be only too pleased to see the back of it. The way I see it you'll be doing them a favour.'

...

'Yes, yes, yes, of course the curator fears for his life. Maybe you haven't offered him enough of the cut for him to overcome his fear. Don't be greedy, Massoud.'

. . .

'I can't see where your risk is, Massoud, you're not even in Iran. And I dare say you won't be visiting again in a hurry either.'

. . .

'Well, I'm getting cold feet on this deal. I thought I was dealing with a man who could perform. Apparently not. Massoud, the next time you call, it will be to tell me when you are delivering. Until then, bye-bye.'

After that incident I started really taking notice of the paintings hanging all over the flat. The famous names were hung in the prominent positions, so that visitors could easily announce their admiration with an 'oh, there's my favourite Dufy, or now that Toulouse–Lautrec really is a find'. The unknowns, bought on spec, were more inaccessible. If they didn't attract interest from visitors they would be banished to a little storeroom, out of which would come the replacements for display. I came to know this because during my tenure as DIY man, changing the paintings was a privilege that Godfrey felt I was responsible enough to handle. I had no idea whether some of the more obscure paintings retrieved from the store had been 'purchased' from countries which had been raped post social upheaval similar to what was being attempted in Iran, or had been 'purchased' by Godfrey at a time of his financial strength from a close friend who owed him a favour and was suffering financial hardship.

Naturally his most significant work was hung in the most prominent position. The painting was a large Renoir. Of course, it could have been a replica, it could have been a fake, and, knowing Godfrey as I was coming to do, it could have been stolen, or to put it nicely, removed from some collection under threat by burning from political or religious zealots in some part of the world. The facts were that it was a Renoir, that he had several other prominent original paintings, and that he wasn't in any way hiding it away or not willing to show it off to any visitor, even if that person should be Sir Napier Featherstonehaugh, the then CEO of Scotland Yard, another of Godfrey's regular visitors.

†††

There had been a water problem in the flat above the sitting room, and Godfrey's ceiling had been slightly damaged. Some of the old lining paper had bubbled and a large patch was discoloured. The dampness had seeped through the ceiling quite close to the painting. Once it had dried out Godfrey asked me to scrape, fill, rub down, patch and finish paint the ceiling, that is, return it to its former glory.

I set to work on the repairs. A few feet from the affected patch was the Renoir. I nervously removed the painting and stood it on the floor in another part of the large room under the cover of a sheet. I meticulously covered the Mackintosh sideboard that was too large to move, and the herringbone light oak floor. I then stripped the damaged lining, rubbed down and began the necessary filling. Then the new lining, feathering it into the good surround. The following day I rubbed down again, primed, and prepared for the finish coat.

A knock on the front door brought Godfrey out of his study. A friend of his wife, a close neighbour at the family home in Kent, was passing by to pick up some goods for Godfrey's wife back home. Accompanying her were two tearaway kids. They shot into the flat, chasing each other round and round the ladder on which I was perched. Godfrey was completely unperturbed by the raucousness, but I had visions of one of the kids setting a foot through the Renoir I'd propped up against the wall. I got off the ladder and replaced the painting on the wall. The dirty renovating work was complete. I figured it was safer up there.

All that remained for me to do was to paint the repaired ceiling. I rolled it once that afternoon, and returned the next morning to give it another coat. When I had finished, I cleaned up and prepared to leave. I was due some money from Godfrey. He was out for a short while so I spent some minutes mooching about the place looking again at the books and little sculptures that were lying about the place in abundance. He was taking longer than I expected and I was getting bored. I began looking at the paintings all over again. This time I was looking at them very closely, the textures, the brush-strokes, the different ways in which the artists applied the paint. I stopped at the Renoir, and was looking very closely at the face of the woman in the centre of the canvas. She appeared to have pimples, rather like little white dots all over her face. I wondered how it was possible to get such fine dots on the painting and more importantly, what was the reason or effect of them. I stood back a little and realised they were not only on the face, they covered the whole painting. A little further back and they were unnoticeable. I went up close again and then I realised they weren't white dots at all, they were magnolia dots. Magnolia was not a colour one would recognize on Renoir's palette, but it was the colour that I'd just finished rolling on the ceiling.

The hair on the back of my neck leapt erect. My mouth went dry. I broke out in a cold sweat. My first reaction was one of needing to get out of there. Escape. I then became more rational. Could I fix the problem? Remove the dots? Each one? Two million dots? No way. *En masse*? Like take a cloth of turps and rub them off? I imagined taking a cloth of turps and wiping a Renoir. No. Crazy. Those little dots were there to stay. I could rely on only one aspect of the saga to save my bacon. That was that no-one would notice, or if they did, no-one would be able to work out what they were or how the hell they got there.

Godfrey's hand was on the door. Breezing in, he asked: 'Are you alright? You're awfully pale.'

'A little faint,' I said, 'I was just leaving, I'll be better out in the open.'

'Fine,' he said, 'thanks very much, you've done a first-rate job. You never said you were a skilled painter as well as carpenter.'

'Renoir's the painter,' I said, 'I just dabble.'

Godfrey laughed, I gulped for air and left.

I was getting near the end of my stay at Mr.Bowman's fantastic penthouse. The spare-room cupboards were almost complete. He was having a final push on all the other bits and pieces that make up such an extraordinary abode. And on one particular Friday there was a full complement of works-people servicing the machine that was the great man's existence. Mick Meehan, the Irish plumber, was upgrading the kitchen taps and servicing the geyser. Linda Blignaut, an Afrikaans girl from a small rural town in South Africa called Bronkhorstspruit was hanging curtains that she had custom made. Stephen Parrott, an antique restorer, was assisting me with the staining to match of the oak cupboards. A lady called Angelique, a regular from 'The Flower Pot' had come in to do the flowers. And off course the ever faithful maid Mrs. Maria de Diaz was still in making sure nothing went awry.

Godfrey came through to where I was working. He was leaving for the weekend to the family pad in Kent. Mrs. de Diaz was also sailing off. He was in high spirits. He'd left a bottle of champers in the fridge and put me in charge of decanting for the staff to enjoy when they took a lunch-break. Thanks very much we all said, and he was gone.

Lunch-break arrived, all the service agents came together with an assortment of eating arrangements which ranged from me with nothing to Mick Meehan with a Tupperware the size of a small suitcase from which emerged a three course meal topped by a supersized Bar-One. I went off for the champers, was surprised on opening the fridge at the sight of two bottles, grabbed one and returned to the comrade workers. All assembled for their glass of champers, duly burped their appreciation and that was that. Or so I thought.

On Monday morning Godfrey fairly pounced on me as I arrived at the door. He was trying to look angry.

'You know that bottle of champagne on Friday…' he started.

'Yes, sir, everyone says to thank you very much,' I said.

'Did you not notice there were two bottles in the fridge?'

'Yes, I did, but we only had one,' I said, realizing there was a problem and providing a pre-emptive defence to what I thought the problem might be.

'Well you took the wrong bottle.' He stopped, allowing that to sink in. 'Does that mean anything to you? I tried to phone but you weren't answering, I thought of coming back but I knew it would already be too late.'

'I'm not with you sir,' I said, genuinely bemused.

'Let me spell it out for you in plain English then, my boy. There were two bottles in the fridge, one a no-name brand from Tesco that was meant for you. And a bottle of Dom Perignon that survived the Second World War. I managed to lay my hands on it – me and Margaret Thatcher who also got one and I believe Ronald Reagan got two. There are a few others scattered around the globe. It cost me $500. And you drank it.'

'I'm very sorry,' I said, amused but showing horror and remorse.

'And the thing that hurt me most,' continued our Godfrey, 'was that I knew not one goddamned one of you would be able to appreciate what it was you were drinking.'

I thought back to the Friday luncheon, and remembered Linda Blignaut, the girl from Bronkhorstspruit, commenting that she thought the champagne was quite good. 'Quite tit,' was the expression she used, but I didn't tell Godfrey that.

Tim outside Harrods, Knightsbridge having just completed decorating Mr. Phulls flat. The holdall contained LP records.

BIBLIOGRAPHY:

Anderson, John Lee, Che Guevara, bantam books, 1997.

Breytenbach, Breyten, The True Confessions of an Albino Terrorist, Faber and Faber, 1984.

Buchan, John, Gordon at Khartoum, Davies, 1934.

Carver, Raymond, the Stories of Raymond Carver, Picador, 1985.

Coetzee, J., M., Disgrace, Vintage, 2000.

Crampton, Hazel, The sunburnt Queen, Jacana, 2004.

Dawkins, Richard, The God Delusion, Black Swan, 2006.

Eliot, Sian, Family Archive-Jimmy Eliot. Kind permission.

Fifty Mutinies, Rebellions and Revolutions, Oldham Press, Undated.

Foote, Geoffrey, The Labour Party's Political Thought. Croom Helm, 1986.

Gevisser, Mark, Lost and Found in Johannesburg, Jonathan Ball, 2014.

Geyser, O., Jan Smuts and his International Contemporaries, Covos Day, 2001.

Gladwell, Malcolm, Blink, Penguin, 2005.

Haynes, Letitia, The Buried Past in Family History, The Book Guild, 1993.

Haynes, Tim, The House at the Edge of the World, M&G, 2001.

Haynes, Harry Walter, letters and papers, Self, 1900-1960.

Hitchens, Christopher, Hitch 22, Atlantic, 2010.

Hyslop, Jonathan, The Notorious Syndicalist, Jacana, 2004.

Malan, Rian, Resident Alien, Jonathan Ball, 2009.

Moss, Glenn, The New Radicals, Jacana, 2014.

Pakenham, Thomas, The Boer War, Abacus, 1992.

Pakenham, Thomas, The Scramble for Africa, Jonathan Ball, 1991.

Reitz, Denys, Adrift on the Open Veld, Faber and Faber, 1999.

Roth, Philip, Exit Ghost, Vintage, 2007.

Roth, Philip, The Dying Animal, Vintage books, 2006.

Rushdie, Salman, Joseph Anton, Jonathan Cape, 2012.

Rushdie, Salman, Midnights Children, vintage books, 2006.

Smuts, J., C., Holism and Evolution, N&S Press, 1926.

Steel, Mark, Reasons to be Cheerful, Scribner, 2001.

Vonnegut, Kurt, A Man without a Country, Bloomsbury, 2006.

Wikipedia – of course, when all else failed.

Photographs.

© Haynes Family Archives.

© Whitehead, Brian – Images and typography, Kind Permission, 1976 & 2015.

Siblings 2006: Tacye Dedwith (Dedwith Group of Companies), Sheilagh Stephens (Parys Business woman), Tim Haynes (author), Terrence Haynes (President Macdonalds UK).

For Terence...

I walked the Robberg today.
To the small island.

Like we did.

There are boardwalks now, to shield from harm.
There were no paths when we walked it. Remember?
We were free then, our journey about to begin.

The sun was bright, balmy, no cloud to blunt its ray.
The sky was blue, a blue that defined blue.
Vast swells rolled in silently rising up
in white anger to pound musselled rock
leaving spray cascading through fissured coal.

Like it was.

Is the memory of that just locked-up
or
has it left like a bird from a broken nest?

Can we recall that image and its promise
Bask in the warmth of reminiscence
Hope against hope that we might stave off the gloom of loss
As the sun begins to set and darkness shrouds
the last chimera of a life discharged yet incomplete.

Tim.

GLOSSARY OF TERMS:

'Fok daardie Hottentot, laat hom val, dan is daar een minder.' *– Fuck the Hottentot, let him fall, then there is one more less.*

'Roufs' *– (scabs).*

'Sy's a kleurling' *– she is a person of mixed race.*

'Tas' *– Tassenberg wine (sold very cheaply by the bottle and the flagon).*

'Tsay' *– that's it!*

'Sy moet dink a bietjie further, the rubbish.' *– She needs to think a little further, she is trash.*

Angola *– Country north west of South Africa.*

Athol Fugard *– a South African playwright, novelist, actor, and director who writes in English.*

Atlantis *– new township built on the Cape Flats.*

Bargees *- people forced to work on barges in England 19thC*

Battles of Elandslaagte *– was a battle of the Second Boer War, and one of the few clear-cut tactical victories won by the British during that conflict.*

Battles of Lombard's Kop *– was one of the early engagements of the Second Boer War.*

Battles of Paardeberg *– a major battle during the Second Anglo-Boer War. Fought near Paardeberg Drift on the banks of the Modder River in the Orange Free State near Kimberley.*

Battles of Poplar Grove *– on 7 March 1900 followed on from the Relief of Kimberley during the Second Boer War as the British army moved to take the Boer capital of Bloemfontein.*

Benoni *– is a city on the East Rand near Johannesburg, in the South African province of Gauteng.*

Berea *– a suburb close to the centre of Johannesburg.*

Betogers *– Protesters.*

Birnam *– suburb in Johannesburg.*

Black doek thing *– black cloth head dress or scarf.*

Bloemfontein *– city in the Orange Free State if South Africa.*

Blombos *– Blombos Cave on the southern Cape Coast, 300km east of Cape Town.*

Blotto *– drunk.*

Boykie *– a lad.*

Braai *– barbecue.*

Bronkhorstspruit *– is a small developing town 50 km east of Pretoria, Gauteng, South Africa.*

Calvinia *– is a regional town in the Northern Cape province of South Africa named after the French religious reformer Jean Calvin.*

Cape Flats – *is an expansive, low-lying, sandy, wind swept, flat area situated to the southeast of the central business district of Cape Town.*

Chataysim – *a Yiddish word for Afrikaners in South Africa.*

Clarendon Circle – *a main road intersection in the suburb of Hilbrow in Johannesburg.*

Colesberg – *a classic Karoo town in the Cape - half way between Johannesburg and Cape Town.*

Coloureds – *a term for being of mixed race in South Africa.*

Colonel Denys Reitz – *historicaly a prominent Boer leader and Smuts' right hand man.*

Corlett Drive – *a main road in Johannesburg.*

Cradle of Humankind – *a World Heritage Site first named by UNESCO in 1999, about 50 kilometres northwest of Johannesburg, South Africa.*

Crown Mines – *one of the richest gold mines the world has ever known near Johannesburg.*

Currie Cup – *South Africa's premier domestic rugby competition.*

Dagga joints – *a strain of marijuana.*

Dale Carnegie – *an American writer and lecturer and the developer of famous courses in self-improvement.*

De Aar – *the second-most important railway junction in the country, situated on the line between Cape Town and Kimberley.*

Deep kak – *deep shit.*

Devil's Peak – *is part of the mountainous backdrop to Cape Town city.*

Die Stem – *the national anthem of South Africa from 1957 to 1994.*

Drive-in – *a form of cinema structure consisting of a large outdoor movie screen, a projection booth, a concession stand and a large parking area for automobiles.*

Dundee – *a town in Kwazulu Natal.*

Fenians – *was an umbrella term for the Fenian Brotherhood and Irish Republican Brotherhood (IRB).*

Finsbury Park – *a suburb and a large green space in central north of London.*

Ford Zephyr – *a British car manufactured by the Ford Motor Company in the United Kingdom.*

Fordsburg – *a suburb of Johannesburg, South Africa and a major centre of Indian and Pakistani culture.*

Ganja – *cannabis, or commonly known as marijuana.*

Git – *idiot or asshole.*

Grootfontein – *translates as 'Large Spring' after the nearby hot springs, is a city in the Otjozondjupa Region of central Namibia.*

Harfield Village – *is a suburb in the south of Cape Town.*

Head honcho – leader, top dog.

Hillbrow – *is an inner city residential neighbourhood of Johannesburg.*

Houghton – *is a wealthy suburb of Johannesburg, where Nelson Mandella lived after the 1994 election took place.*

Internationale – *is a widely-sung left-wing anthem.*

Jameson Raid – *a botched raid on Paul Kruger's Transvaal Republic carried out by a British colonial statesman Leander Starr Jameson and his Company of mercenaries.*

Johannes Balthazar Vorster – *served as the Prime Minister of South Africa from 1966 to 1978 and as the fourth State President of South Africa from 1978 to 1979. He was pro-Nazi in spirit and a complete dictatorial neo-facist.*

Khaki shorts – *trousers in a light shade of yellow-brown. Khaki is a loanword incorporated from Hindustani (meaning 'soil-colored') and is originally derived from the Persian: (Khâk, literally meaning 'soil'), which came to English from British India via the British Indian Army.*

King Moshoeshoe – *a minor chief of the Bamokoteli lineage and due to attacks Moshoeshoe to move his settlement to the Qiloane plateau. The name was later changed to Thaba Bosiu or 'mountain of the night' in Lesotho.*

Klap – *hit, assault.*

Kombi – *known officially as the Volkswagen Transporter – Kombi or Microbus.*

Kosher – *Food that may be consumed according to halakha (Jewish law) is termed kosher in English, from the Ashkenazi pronunciation of the Hebrew term kashér, meaning 'fit' (in this context, fit for consumption).*

Kraaifontein – *a suburb of Cape Town.*

Kugel – *a materialistic, wannabe-sexy Jewish woman who belongs to a specific subculture of wealth and style, with affected mannerisms and a nasal way of talking. The term is used by both Jews and Gentiles in South Africa, and even by kugels themselves.*

Ladysmith – *a city in the Uthukela District of KwaZulu-Natal, South Africa, which is 230 kilometres north-west of Durban.*

Lesotho – *an enclaved landlocked country completely surrounded by South Africa, with a population slightly over two million people.*

Llandudno – *a residential suburb of Cape Town.*

Lombard's Kop – *one of two British defeats around Ladysmith that came to be known as 'Mournful Monday', or the battle of Ladysmith.*

Louis Botha Avenue – *an old main road leading from Johannesburg toward Pretoria city.*

Lourenco Marques – *a city now called Maputo which is the capital city of Mozambique.*

Magaliesburg – *the Magaliesberg is mountain range which is visible to the* *north and west of Johannesburg. Burg is the Afrikaans name for mountain.*

Mal – *mad.*

Maputo – *originally called Lourenco Marques.*

Middelburg – *a large farming and industrial town in the South African province of Mpumalanga.*

Mitchell's Plain – *a largely coloured township about 32 km from the city of Cape Town.*

MPLA – *a radical socialist movement that epitomised the heroism of African liberation, under Agostinho Neto, the first president of independent Angola.*

Nogal – *Afrikaans for: what is more or moreover.*

Observatory – *a suburb in Johannesburg's east; it borders the suburbs of Houghton Estate, Cyrildene, Linksfield, Bellevue, Bellevue East and Dewetshof. It is the city's highest point.*

Okavango swamps – *in Botswana is a large inland delta formed where the Okavango River reaches a tectonic trough in the central part of the endorheic basin of the Kalahari.*

Okhela – *an unsettling story that involved Bryten Brytenbach that sadly does not fit easily into the dominant narrative of the South African struggle for liberation.*

Ou manne – *old men – soldiers who have sreved their time.*

Soutpiele – *(vulgar, army slang) A South African with British heritage. So named for having one foot in South Africa, one foot in Britain and his penis dangling in the Atlantic.*

Ovambo – *ethnic groups which inhabit Owamboland in northern Namibia as well as the southernmost Angolan province Cunene.*

P. W. Botha – *another leader of South Africa from 1978 to 1989, serving as Prime Minister from 1978 to 1984 and the first executive State President from 1984 to 1989. He was a pro-Nazi in and a complete dictatorial neo-facist while he governed.*

Poesboek – *soft porn picture story book – cheap trashy romantic magazine.*

Quick toot – *quick tug at the alcohol bottle.*

Rockspider – *English exprssion for Afrikaner.*

Rookers – *smokers usually dagga joints or marijuana.*

Rundu – *town in northern Namibia, on the border with Angola.*

Siege of Kimberley – *took place during the Second Boer War at Kimberley, Cape Colony (present-day South Africa), when Boer forces from the Orange Free State and the Transvaal besieged the diamond mining town.*

Slammer – *gaol or jail.*

Sophiatown – *a suburb of Johannesburg. Sophiatown was a legendary black cultural hub that was destroyed under Apartheid, rebuilt* *under the name of Triomf, and in 2006 officially returned to its original name.*

Steve Biko – *a student leader, who founded the Black Consciousness Movement which would empower and mobilize much of the urban black population. Since his death in police custody, he has been called a martyr of the anti-Apartheid movement.*

Stoep – *a raised veranda in front of a house (Afrikaans and Dutch).*

Strandfontein – *a settlement in the Western Cape.*

Thaba Bosiu – *a sandstone plateau in Lesotho, used as a stronghold, acting as a formed and natural fortress where the Basotho people gathered to take refuge during times of war.*

The Rand Revolt – *an armed uprising of white miners in the Witwatersrand region of South Africa, in March 1922.*

Tjommies – *alternative form of chums or friends.*

Triomf – *see Sophiatown also known as Sof'town or Kofifi, is a suburb of Johannesburg.*

Troepies – *a divergent group of soldiers, from officers to ordinary foot soldiers in the South African army.*

Vrot drunk – *rotten drunk.*

WASP bullies – *White Anglo-Saxon Protestant bullies.*

Witbank – *a city situated on the Highveld of Mpumalanga, South Africa. The name Witbank is Afrikaans for White Ridge and is named after a white sandstone outcrop where wagon transport drivers rested. The city is known for the coal-mining in the surrounding region.*

Witwatersrand – *a 56 km long north facing scarp in the Gauteng Province of South Africa. It consists of a hard, erosion resistant quartzite sedimentary rock, over which several north-flowing rivers form waterfalls, which account for the name 'Witwatersrand' meaning the 'ridge of white waters' in Afrikaans.*

Yeoville – *a suburb of Johannesburg, it is curently a community of migrants, mostly economic migrants from all over the country and the rest of Africa. It is a vibrant, colourful, often chaotic pan-African area.*

Yok – *Jewish term for Christian.*

Youngsfield Military Camp – *situated in Cape Town.*

Ysterplaat – *an airbase of the South African Air Force, located in Cape Town.*

...now collecting more
'MISFIT'
stories for the next one...